OUT WINDHAM WAY

A Photographic Tour of
Windham, Ashland, Prattsville,
Maplecrest & Hensonville, 1890-1945

OUT WINDHAM WAY

A Photographic Tour of Windham, Ashland, Prattsville, Maplecrest & Hensonville, 1890-1945

LARRY TOMPKINS

Larry J. Tompkins

BLACK · DOME

www.blackdomepress.com

Published by Black Dome Press Corp.
649 Delaware Ave., Delmar, N.Y. 12054
blackdomepress.com
(518) 439-6512

First Edition Paperback 2014

ISBN: 978-1-883789-75-6

Library of Congress Control Number: 2014951601

This book was made possible in part with support from the Windham Chapter of the Catskill Mountain Foundation.

All of the illustrations in this book are from the collection of Larry Tompkins.

The dated excerpts in this book are from past issues of the *Windham Journal* and are used with permission.

Front cover: O. R. Coe's Windham Hotel, present site of Key Bank, Village of Windham. Negative, circa 1881.

Design: Toelke Associates, www.toelkeassociates.com

Printed in the USA

10 9 8 7 6 5 4 3 2 1

Dedication

In a very small community like ours, heritage is tangible; it is something you can touch, if only the faded tombstone in the cemetery, something you can almost feel in the air because it is all around you. Fortunately a record of our heritage is available in the writings of the early historians, in later family histories, and in photos that allow us to glimpse the past and remember and share in the lives of our ancestors.

In Dedication to
Shawn and Danielle

Never forget!

Welcome to Windham

It is a work day in 1895 and dozens of businesses keep their proprietors in town tending their stores—Osborn's Grist Mill, Atwater's Hardware, Mrs. Wood's Millinery, Harry Miller's Department Store, Mott's Drug Store, and the always very busy Brockett & Sons grocery and dry goods store. For the many farmers on the outskirts of the village, the day starts early and ends late.

We thought it would be nice to greet you from our small farm in Mitchell Hollow. I am Burton Robinson, and this is my wife Meuta Ann. We welcome you to our beautiful mountaintop community. There are many places to see and stories to tell. The people are friendly, the food is good, and the scenery is spectacular. So, please, stay a while as our guests.

Contents

Foreword

There is no shortage of history books in the world. Every child who has ever set foot in any kind of classroom has, at one time or another, been the caretaker of any number of thick volumes that recount the passage of time, the shifting social landscape and the changes that are an accepted part of life.

When asked what constitutes a history book, most will think of complex, life-altering events—world wars, economic upheavals, royal successions, and political transformations—that fill the pages of most texts focusing on history.

And yet, sometimes history can be as simple as a postcard.

For decades the *Windham Journal* has highlighted our own local history on its "Looking Back" page. This popular weekly segment features text culled from past issues and a photograph of a bygone era, usually supplied by the mountaintop's own Larry Tompkins.

It was more than twenty years ago that Larry first came to the *Windham Journal* office to both introduce himself to the new editor (i.e., yours truly) and offer his amazingly comprehensive collection of photographs and postcards to supplement our page. That he knew the area was never a question. A native of Windham, his roots go deep and his love for the mountaintop—its people and its remarkable landscape and structures—is evident in every caption he writes.

Week after week, month after month, and indeed year after year, Larry has provided so much more than just a picture or a postcard. With each envelope stuffed with historic trivia he hands me, he gives us all a glimpse into the life of those who lived, loved and worked the land.

Truesdell Sawmill and 1912 automobile, Lexington.

Larry's collection of photos and postcards is truly amazing. Yet, it is the information he supplies with each one that makes it so much more than just a moment in time caught on camera. Through his captions, he introduces us to families, farms, businesses and houses that, without these pictures, would have disappeared from memory. Time does indeed march on, and what was once thought to be constant has often been replaced by new structures—new stores, restaurants or homes. But when Larry asks us to "look back" at scenes from East Windham, Hensonville, Big Hollow or Red Falls, we do so armed with information and insight into the lives we're seeing. What was once static becomes so much more dynamic.

You might think, perhaps, that after all the years of publishing a picture once a week, at some point the historical well would run dry. You would be wrong. With what seems to be an unending and fascinating supply, Larry keeps providing new and wonderful scenes to share with our readers.

Wallace and Emma Cammer and son Sheridan, Prattsville, 1914.

There are probably many who remember when Sokoll's Garage was on Main Street. Others still speak of the start of the ski industry at Cave Mountain. Often these photos and captions spark conversations that begin with the words, "I remember when ... " and it is, without a doubt, the thorough and entertaining information contained in each caption that draws people in. Whether the photo or postcard dates back to the late nineteenth century or a mere fifty or sixty years, the insights provided go far beyond the simple "who, what, when and where." It's not just a picture of a drug store in town, it's a wonderful peek into the world of Harry "Doc" Avery—standing behind the counter of obviously well-stocked shelves, ready to assist any and all customers.

Elgin Creamery, Village of Windham, 1902.

Mad Brook Flood, Village of Windham, 1895.

This book is the culmination of years of research, as well as Larry's unflagging enthusiasm for the subject. This visual record of drover's taverns, small family farms, boardinghouses and historic buildings is as entertaining as it is informative. Yet, beyond the brick, mortar and wood are the generations of people who came, settled, lived and prospered on the mountaintop.

Thanks to Larry Tompkins's years of dedicated work, they will never be forgotten.

—Lori Anander, Editor, *Windham Journal*, October 2014

Cook and Haney Carpenters and Builders, Hensonville, circa 1892.

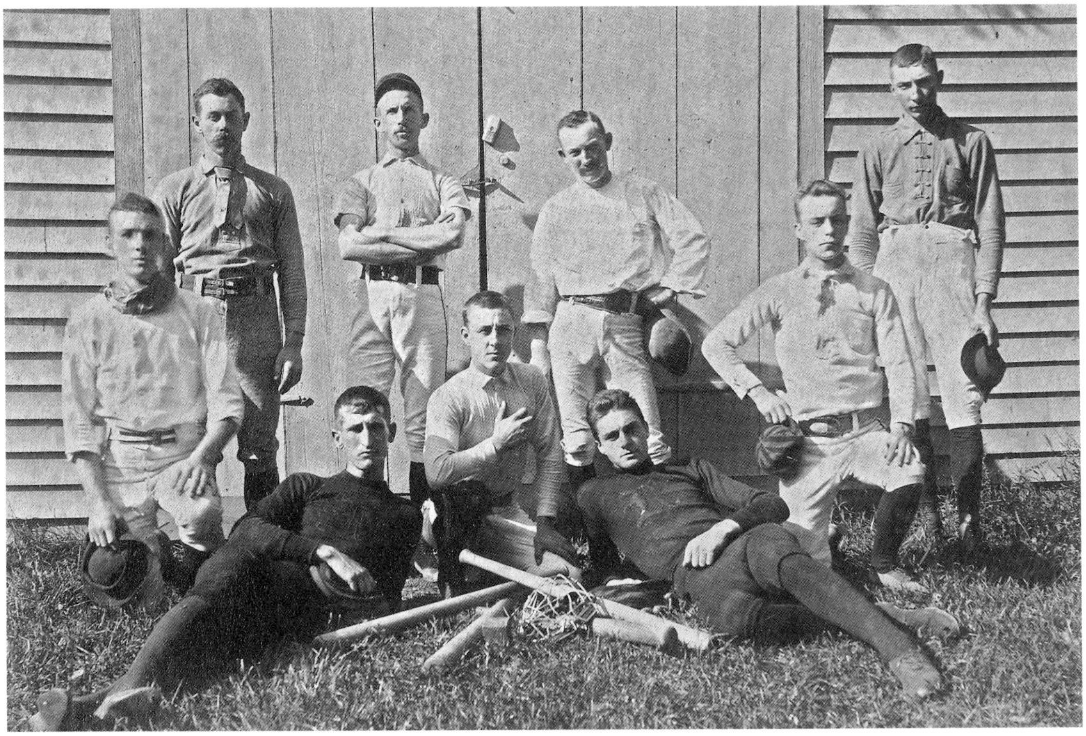

Windham Baseball Team, 1890.

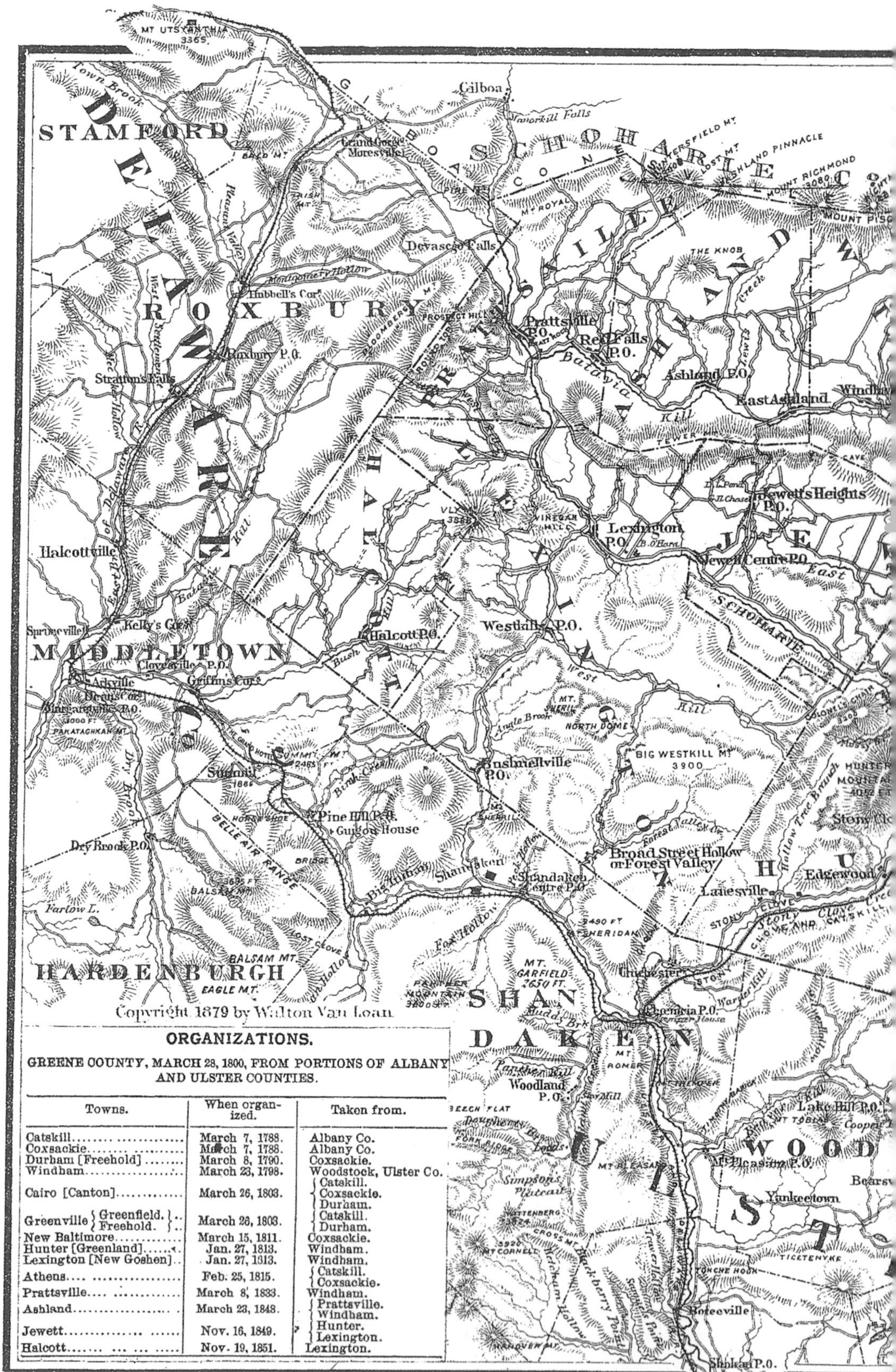

Copyright 1879 by Walton Van Loan.

ORGANIZATIONS.

GREENE COUNTY, MARCH 28, 1800, FROM PORTIONS OF ALBANY AND ULSTER COUNTIES.

Towns.	When organized.	Taken from.
Catskill	March 7, 1788.	Albany Co.
Coxsackie	March 7, 1788.	Albany Co.
Durham [Freehold]	March 8, 1790.	Coxsackie.
Windham	March 23, 1798.	Woodstock, Ulster Co.
Cairo [Canton]	March 26, 1803.	Catskill. Coxsackie. Durham.
Greenville { Greenfield. Freehold. }	March 26, 1803.	Catskill. Durham.
New Baltimore	March 15, 1811.	Coxsackie.
Hunter [Greenland]	Jan. 27, 1813.	Windham.
Lexington [New Goshen]	Jan. 27, 1813.	Windham.
Athens	Feb. 25, 1815.	Catskill. Coxsackie.
Prattsville	March 8, 1833.	Windham.
Ashland	March 23, 1848.	Prattsville. Windham.
Jewett	Nov. 16, 1849.	Hunter. Lexington.
Halcott	Nov. 19, 1851.	Lexington.

MAP OF
GREENE CO. N.Y.
AND PORTIONS OF
ULSTER AND DELAWARE
COS N.Y.
Scale 3 Miles to the inch
Engraved by J.B. Beers & Co. 36 Vesey St. New York
COXSACKIE
ATHENS
CATSKILL
CAIRO
SAUGERTIES
NEW BALTIMORE
Hudson
Germantown
Tivoli
Stockport
Catskill Station
HUDSON RIVER
RAIL ROAD

Acknowledgments

My first endeavor into recording the history of many Catskill Mountain communities began with Muriel Pons. Besides providing a wealth of knowledge on Prattsville's history, she led me to many longtime residents and their collections of family pictures, which I used for slide presentations on the history of Prattsville.

That beginning led me to other mountaintop families too numerous to name, but to whom I am extremely grateful for their help. Families who did not know who I was, openly and with much joy, shared their personal histories in words and photos so that their families' legacies might be preserved for future generations. To all of them, thank you.

My thanks to Debbie Allen, the past owner of Black Dome Press, for encouraging me to write my own book after my having provided photos for so many other authors' historical books.

Thanks to Steve Hoare, the present owner and editor of Black Dome Press for all of his help and patience in producing this beautiful book, and to Ron Toelke and Barbara Kempler-Toelke for their excellent design.

A special thanks to Lori Anander, editor of the *Windham Journal*, for gracing this book with a foreword. Lori knows me better than most, and there was never any doubt that it should be her words to introduce mine.

A special thanks to Mara Lehmann, who had to live through the production of this book and who typed every word using her uncanny ability to decipher my penmanship! Knowing my love for the mountaintop, Mara was steadfast in her assistance, performing countless hours of proofreading and providing constant encouragement.

This book was made possible in part through the efforts of Phyllis Parrish and the financial support of the Windham Chapter of the Catskill Mountain Foundation. Phyllis Parrish truly believes in and works for the future of Windham and the past that helped shape it. The foundation works year-round in its efforts to improve the lives of people on the mountaintop.

Introduction

"If you are lucky enough to live in the mountains, you are lucky enough."

It's 1960 and I'm on my way to Lawyersville from college in Troy to spend the weekend with my Uncle Lloyd and Aunt Fannie Spaulding on their farm. Sunday morning is here and, although it is a day of rest, the cows still have to be milked before the rest of the day can be enjoyed with a Sunday drive or a visit with friends and relatives. Uncle Lloyd would often suggest that we go "out Windham way," where we have many family members, my home. This book has been thirty-six years in the making while living *Out Windham Way*.

It was thirty-six years ago that the first thoughts of the importance of my own family's heritage dawned on me. I wanted to know more about the mountaintop communities that my ancestors called home since first arriving in 1810. I have learned that to have grown up in or to have lived most or all of your life in a small town in the mountains is truly a blessing. In my own children's generation, most have moved away to make their way in the world, but they will always have the mountaintop to remember and return to.

In 1998 the Town of Windham celebrated 200 years. The township in 1798 consisted of all seven towns on the mountaintop—today's towns of Ashland, Windham, Jewett, Prattsville, Hunter, Lexington, and Halcott. Two hundred years is indeed something to celebrate, but it is really not a long time at all, just a few generations. Longtime residents and natives of the mountaintop can relate through their ancestors to the earliest days of settlement and visualize through

Fire House (left), Hardware Store (right), Village of Windham, circa 1920.

Harry Brockett's son Donavan, age 3, Village of Windham, circa 1904.

Howard & Inez Clarke house, Ashland, circa 1910.

pictures and stories how far we have come in 200 years—from a vast wilderness of haunting woods, mountain lions and wolves, to the quaint little villages of today's Windham, Ashland, and Prattsville. In those 200 years the area saw an extensive tanning industry and manufacturing era in the early to mid-1800s. The tanning industry eventually gave way to dairy farming, which in turn gradually gave way to a major summer and winter resort area attracting tens of thousands of visitors to our mountaintop communities every year.

Early settlers came to the mountains to start a new life on virgin land they could call their own. While using the natural resources of water and timber to make a living in a very rugged area, these early settlers and their children never lost sight of the beauty of the surroundings in which they lived.

So, thirty-six years ago I began to look into the history of the mountaintop.

One of the very early settlers who loved Old Windham and the people he served was Reverend Henry Hedges Prout (1810–1879). In Prout's later years he realized that no written account of the early pioneer days had been put to paper. Recognizing the importance of who these people were, where they came from and what they had endured, Prout began to collect as much information of the early days as he could from the pioneers themselves.

John and Lilly Oliver's daughter Nora, Hensonville, circa 1905.

From February 1869 through March 1870, a series of extensive articles under the heading "Old Times in Windham" was published in the *Windham Journal.* In many cases these articles were first-hand accounts of the early days, circa 1800, when Old Windham was a vast wilderness of dense forests and wild animals. There were no cleared roads, only Indian hunting paths and animal herd paths through the woods. These paths were eventually widened to allow wagons to enter the mountains, establishing small settlements along the way. The stories that Rev. Prout sets forth are some of the earliest first-hand written accounts of life in Old Windham.

Another historian who was eager to record those early days was John Lorton, who in 1886 traveled through Windham, stopping at every home and business in the township. Lorton was sixty-six at the time and knew many of the early pioneers. He wanted to gather as much historical information about each house as he could. These, too, became very extensive articles published in the *Windham Journal* over a year's time. The articles are a wonderful source of very detailed information about life in early Windham.

As you have most likely gathered, far and away the greatest source of mountaintop history since 1857 has been, and still is, the *Windham Journal.* The *Journal* is a weekly look at the lives of local citizens and the events in their community that help shape their community life. Lori Anander, our current long-time editor, and her "family" of local correspondents have done well in maintaining this tradition. Jim Planck, a regular contributor to the *Journal*, writes articles about long-lost historical events that are always fascinating. Another regular contributor is Michael Ryan, who always manages to find fascinating angles in stories on modern-day businesses, events, and people. For good reason, the *Windham Journal* is the oldest published newspaper in New York State operating continuously under the same name.

But, with all this written history, what did Windham, Ashland, and Prattsville look like in 1890? And so my quest for old postcards began about thirty-four years ago. Postcards were an advertisement for just about anything back in 1905. You could even have your own photo put on a card and mailed to anywhere in the country.

I still collect postcards, but after thirty-four years it has become difficult to come across anything new. This is good in one respect, as the same postcards bought thirty years ago for two to four dollars might cost twenty-five dollars each today.

Then I had the idea that I wanted to share these images with the residents of each town, but I didn't have enough material. Thus began a long endeavor to collect photographs of the mountaintop circa 1900, a quest that continues to this day. I found that visiting residents with old family names brings instant gratification to them as they talk about the old days. They are eager to show me old photos of their families and life on the mountaintop. Without exception the hundreds of residents I have visited with personally or on the phone have graciously shared stories and loaned me photos and albums so that I might make slides of their photographs to be shared with each mountaintop community. The pleasure I have gotten from presenting dozens of slide shows over the years comes from seeing the joy on the faces of all those eager to remember.

Two ladies who stand out in my quest for history are Miss Dorothy Talmadge and Mrs. Mary Benham Snow Wooley. Mary would have liked my including "Benham" in her name. Dorothy was a very sharp woman even into her nineties and loved to visit and tell stories for hours. I spoke at length with both ladies in the 1970s and 1980s, trying to learn as much as they knew. Of course, I came up short. There is a big difference between *knowing* history and *living* history as these ladies did. It was both very informative and sometimes amusing to listen to them. With the utmost respect I would say that each thought that she was the matriarch of local history. In speaking to either one I had to be careful not to mention the other's name, which could bring a sharp retort (as I quickly learned). To say that both women were fiercely proud of their heritage on the mountaintop is an understatement.

Dorothy's father, Benjamin Talmadge, was a very popular, involved and influential man about Windham. He seemed to belong to every organization and was on the board of most. As the town lawyer, he knew everyone and learned a lot about Windham's history from his clients. Fortunately,

Above: Dorothy Talmadge, age 16. Photograph circa 1910. Left: Claude Campbell, William Campbell, and Mary Benham Snow. Photograph circa 1910.

Benjamin saved everything. Many years ago I was lucky to be around to rescue his records from what unfortunately becomes the ready repository of most family records—the town landfill.

Mary Wooley had a slight advantage over Dorothy, as her family dates back to at least 1793 on the mountaintop. That is the year when her great-great-grandfather, Dr. Thomas Benham, came to Old Windham from Connecticut. He was the first doctor on the mountaintop. His family lived, at various times, in Prattsville, Lexington, Ashland, and Windham.

In Mary's later years she had but one mission—that the residents of the mountaintop know of their own heritage and the early history of the mountaintop. To this end, along with the help of Olive N. Woodworth and publisher Charles Dornbush of Hope Farm Press, the words of Henry Hedges Prout were put in book form, straight from the pages of the *Windham Journal*. In the late 1960s Mary worked tirelessly on her extensive research into the lives of the families brought to life in Henry's writing.

Mary also wanted to create an addendum to the book with additional information on locations and time periods for homes and businesses mentioned in the articles. This was done, but ended up being very extensive. Unfortunately, thanks to severe editing by the publisher, much crucial information was left out, causing more confusion in an accompanying map. I have many of Mary's original hand-written and typed notes, as well as photos, to help better understand and clarify these early writings. The book was published only once, in 1970, and is now hard to come by.

This book is not intended to be a comprehensive, in-depth look into the history of the mountaintop, for that has already been done. The photos you are about to see are a visual record of the lives our ancestors lived so many years ago.

When I look at the pictures in this book, I am struck by the splendor of the street scenes and the family portraits. I wish I could go back in time and live in Windham and experience life then. But, like you, I must be content with living the past through these beautiful photographs and the written words of our forebears.

The impact of Tropical Storm Irene in 2011 was devastating to the mountaintop, both physically and mentally, yet the rebuilding continues. Two hundred years of pride and a sense of belonging have kept the mountaintop alive and growing.

In the following pages our journey into the past will begin. Starting in East Windham we will be traveling west along the Windham Turnpike (Route 23)—in old days referred to as the Mohican Trail—through Windham Village, Red Falls, and Ashland, to Prattsville. There will be side excursions to other settlements, like Hensonville and Big Hollow (Maplecrest). So, sit back, relax, and enjoy the views—our horse and buggy moves very slowly.

East Windham

East Windham in the mid-1800s was one of two gateway communities from the east to the mountaintop region. The other gateway was through Haines Falls, farther south along the escarpment. For many years in the early pioneer days, East Windham was little more than a rest stop after the long, arduous, four-mile climb from the Durham Valley below. The primitive road hugged the side of Windham High Peak at about 2,000 feet elevation, leaving little room for development.

In 1826 the Windham Turnpike was rebuilt, becoming more or less the Route 23 of today. As the road improved over the years, Barney Butts from Jewett saw some promise in this location. In the mid-1840s, Barney packed up his family and moved to this northern ridge of the Catskill Mountains that overlooked a panoramic view of the countryside to the north and east. Barney began to build himself a home and, later, other family members' houses. Each became a boardinghouse, which would eventually make East Windham a very popular boardinghouse community, while remaining small and thus still retaining the beauty of its location.

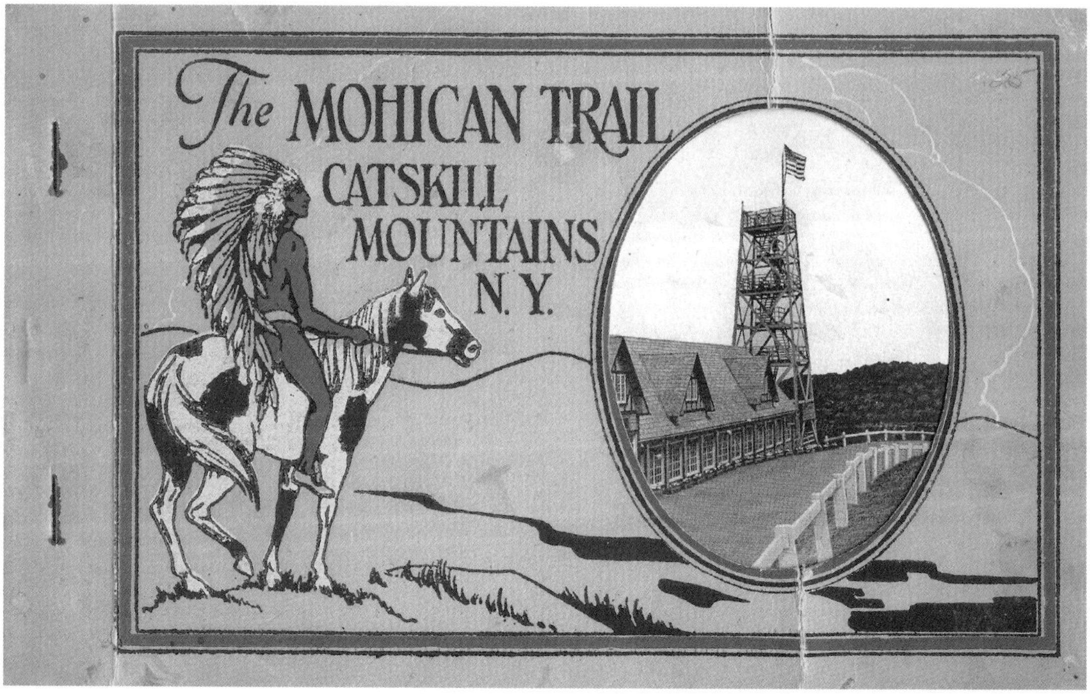

Album Cover for "The Mohican Trail, Catskill Mountains, N.Y.," circa 1945, a souvenir booklet of photographs taken along the Mohican Trail (Route 23) from Catskill to Windham.

The Mohican Indians lived in the upper Hudson Valley for thousands of years. The boundaries of their land were from Lake Champlain in the north to the Catskill Mountains in the south, from the Schoharie Kill in the west to the eastern edge of the Berkshires. They were members of the Algonquian family of tribes. They generally lived in the Hudson Valley, venturing into the Catskills only to hunt. Route 23 probably follows the route of one of those hunting trails, which developed into a turnpike in the early 1800s.

In the late 1800s, as the temperance movement was taking hold, it became quite the event for people from surrounding towns to take a hayride to East Windham for a night in the only town where spirits were available. They might also get a glimpse of a live black bear that the Butts boys trapped and had on display there and at different boardinghouses on the mountaintop.

East Windham expanded to the west along the Mohican Trail, so-named for the former Indian trail that the road roughly followed (and also for marketing purposes, to enhance the romance of coming to the Catskill Mountains). The Mohican Trail itself is a relic of the past. Two hundred and more years ago it was called "The Great Road to the Back Settlements." The "Back Settlements" was the term for what are now Binghamton, Ithaca and other cities in central New York. While the term Mohican Trail is very rarely used today, it is still indicative of the wild high peaks where the Indians once hunted and where many hikers roam today.

Photograph circa 1959. Apparently, unrest amongst "the natives" continued well into the twentieth century. They have gathered at the crest of the Mohican Trail in East Windham to protest the condition of the trail. They were successful, and two years later the road was rebuilt. These young "braves" are, left to right: Peter Mulbury, Jimmy Stead, Tom Martin and Robert Partridge.

Postcard circa 1930. Point Lookout was originally built as Gate's Tea Room circa 1920; it soon became Point Lookout, owned by Mr. and Mrs. Ray French. It became famous for its restaurant, extensive gift shop and 75-foot-high observation tower with a five-state view north and east. Fire destroyed the building in 1965, but it has been rebuilt as a motel and restaurant, minus the observation tower.

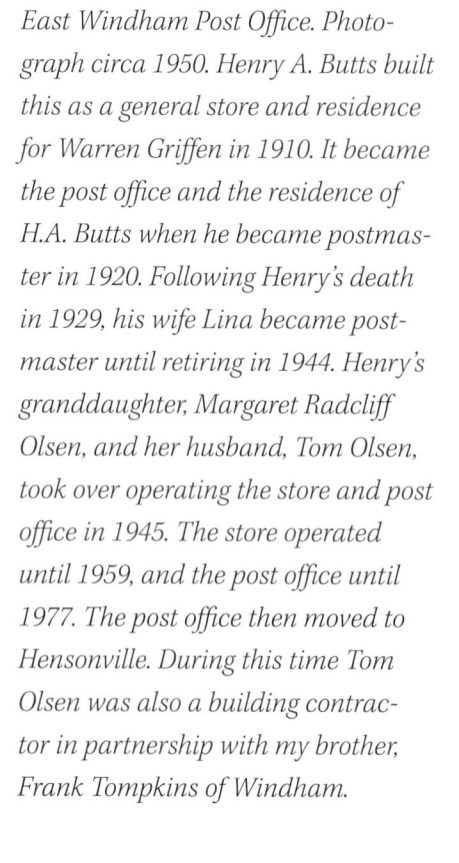

Photograph circa 1910. This is Mount Zoar Villa, a fine resort run by Henry and Lina Butts. It was built around 1890.

East Windham Post Office. Photograph circa 1950. Henry A. Butts built this as a general store and residence for Warren Griffen in 1910. It became the post office and the residence of H.A. Butts when he became postmaster in 1920. Following Henry's death in 1929, his wife Lina became postmaster until retiring in 1944. Henry's granddaughter, Margaret Radcliff Olsen, and her husband, Tom Olsen, took over operating the store and post office in 1945. The store operated until 1959, and the post office until 1977. The post office then moved to Hensonville. During this time Tom Olsen was also a building contractor in partnership with my brother, Frank Tompkins of Windham.

May 1923.

The number of autos that passed through this village Decoration Day over the Mohican Trail, fairly "burned up" the road. Sight seers are amazed at the beautiful scenery along this trail. Why shouldn't they be?

MR. MARK BUTTS
DEALER IN
CATTLE
GREENE COUNTY
East Windham, N. Y. Dec. 31 1907

The Butts Hotel. Postcard circa 1909. This fine hotel was built by Barney Butts's son Isaac in 1878. It was destroyed by fire in 1928 and replaced by a smaller "New Butts Hotel" by Mr. and Mrs. John Barry. It later continued under the ownership of Tom and Margaret Olsen. The Olsens named the hotel The Olcliff. It burned, along with five other buildings, in 1964.

"The Barrymore." Postcard circa 1910. This lovely resort, built and operated by John Barry and his wife Bertha Butts Barry about 1880, continued in operation until 1964 when it burned. At that time the hotel was known as The Parthenon.

View from Mount Zoar looking East over East Windham. Photograph circa 1910. Center right is the Summit House. Center, behind trees, is the "Barrymore," and center left is the Butts Hotel. The building at lower right is the Summit House Amusement Hall. The building opposite Butts Hotel is the Butts Livery.

June 1930.

The Taylors, a well known family of gypsies, who have been coming to this section, off and on for twenty-seven years, arrived here [East Windham] Monday with their saddle horses and house-keeping outfit and are encamped near the school house. They will rent out horses. Mrs. Taylor is one of the best fortune tellers in the state, but is no longer able to give Readings, much to the regret of all who have formerly experienced her unusual powers, owing to the present laws of the state which prohibits practice of the ancient art for money.

Looking East through East Windham. Photograph circa 1920. The landmark stone wall bordering Route 23 on the south side is becoming a long-lost art. The large slabs of stone came from the ledges above the hamlet. The building in center was rebuilt in 1910 and in later years was the home of Thomas and Gladys McDonald. The Mount Zoar Villa is next, at right, and then the East Windham Post Office.

Photograph circa 1890. The Summit House was originally built as the Barney Butts house in 1848. In 1873 it was operated as a boardinghouse by Butts's son-in-law Abbot Lamoreau. Abbot and his partner, Adelbert Chichester, purchased the property for $5,000 and gave it the name Summit House. Abbot greatly expanded the hotel, adding many refinements including a dance hall and bowling alley.

Photograph circa 1910. Another view from Mount Zoar of the Summit House, Amusement Hall and the Annex. Kate Hill is in the background.

August 1882.

Lost from the Summit House, East Windham, a black bear belonging to Barney Butts. He had four legs and three feet, was in good condition though not particularly handsome. Five dollars reward will be paid to any person who will return him safe and sound, and no questions asked—of the bear.

Photograph circa 1885. The East Windham Toll Gate, looking east along present-day Route 23, just before entering the hamlet of East Windham.

This toll gate was erected in 1826 and was one of three between East Windham and Prattsville. They were part of the Schoharie Kill Bridge Company's toll road from South Durham to Roxbury. In 1826 $5,000 was raised by the company to completely rebuild the mountain roadway. It is this route that the present-day roadway follows, although rebuilt again in 1961 to straighten it out a bit more and smooth out some of the turns. Local farmers and tavern owners were hired as path masters to maintain the toll road in their vicinity. For every 10 miles of travel, it cost 12½ ¢ for a wagon and two horses.

This toll gate was operated by the Sherman family for many years. The state took over the road around 1900. Marcus Sherman Jr. built a dance hall in East Windham on the north side of Route 23 above the old toll house in the mid-1920s.

The people, left to right, are: Laura Humphrey, age 15; woman seated, unknown; Marcus Sherman, age 18; woman seated, Madge Austin. The boys are Robert and Clifford Sherman.

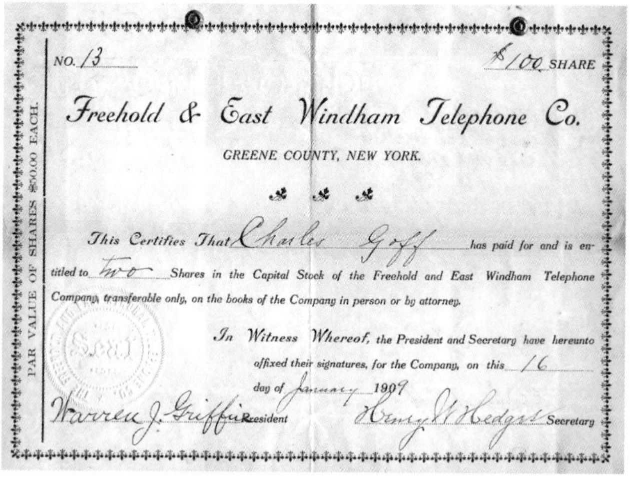
PAR VALUE OF SHARES $50.00 EACH.

NO. 13 $100 SHARE

Freehold & East Windham Telephone Co.

GREENE COUNTY, NEW YORK.

This Certifies That Charles Goff has paid for and is entitled to two Shares in the Capital Stock of the Freehold and East Windham Telephone Company, transferable only, on the books of the Company in person or by attorney.

In Witness Whereof, the President and Secretary have hereunto affixed their signatures, for the Company, on this 16 day of January 1909

Warren J. Griffin President Henry W. Hedges Secretary

August 1927.

The Rainbow Revelers' Orchestra of five pieces: Harry Prandoni, violin; Edwin Mulbury, banjo; George Ratcliff, coronet; Reynold Rusk, drums; Harvey Brockett, piano; are fulfilling engagements three nights a week at Silver Lake where they are otherwise called "The Silver Lake Serenaders."

Boating on Silver Lake. Photograph circa 1915. Thomas St. John came to Windham in 1907 after 26 years teaching at the Browning School for Boys. After becoming a resident, he arranged for a summer place of instruction and recreation on his property in Brooksburg, known as the Cascade Ranch. Later, around 1912, he purchased a property in East Windham and promoted Silver Lake. It became a popular water sports center for locals and city guests. In later years Silver Lake was acquired by the Girls' Vacation Fund as a camp for underprivileged girls from the city.

Union Society

As we travel west a short ways along the Windham Turnpike, we meet up with a road to the right (Old Road), the original turnpike west until 1826. Going west on either road we enter an area known as Union Society, a mixture of homes, farms and boardinghouses since the very early days. Without a source of waterpower, industry did not develop here and the area remained rural. But, it did have its own post office.

The Grassmer. Postcard circa 1895. This is the old Lyman Turk farm, which was sold in 1885 to William Dewell. Dewell was a very prosperous farmer, but it was hard work. He began to think that since everyone else was in the boardinghouse business, why not him? Along with the help of his wife Mary, The Grassmer was born. It was a very big boardinghouse that took the place of the old farmhouse.

In 1911 things changed. An organization called The Society for the Relief of Half Orphans and Destitute Children began bringing children from the city to the Catskills. In 1911 they stayed at George Seeley's Orchard Grove House in Hensonville. The following year the children came to The Grassmer, now run by William's son B.G. Dewell.

At some point early on, Mr. Howell of New York City, a wealthy businessman, purchased The Grassmer for the Orphan Society and the home was named after him—Howell's Holiday Farm.

Why the name Union Society? In an era, circa 1820, when few church buildings existed, the very religious settlers here from New England needed to observe the Lord's day. A private home, a nearby schoolhouse, or even a tavern would be turned into a place of worship for a day, for all denominations to take their turn. Hence the name Union Society. This worked for several decades until congregations grew and proper churches could be built in every village and hamlet.

Cascade Tea Room. Postcard 1941. This house was formerly Mr. St. John's Cascade Ranch for boys. In later years he converted part of the house into a tea room. Mr. St. John was also a pioneer in electrical handicraft and issued books on scientific studies.

Pleasant Home. Photograph circa 1895. This summer resort accommodated a larger number of guests. For thirty-five years David Davis kept updating and expanding his resort, at one time purchasing the Fox Hotel to the east. Hay rides, bowling and other games were popular attractions.

The Union Society Post Office had been here for many years. In 1912 Union Society was renamed Brooksburg. The post office remained here until 1923, when it closed and was moved to East Windham. The house is now long gone. Now this is the site of the Greek Orthodox Church, The Assumption, built in 1961.

Photograph circa 1895. David Davis outside his resort establishment, Pleasant Home, in Union Society. Davis raised a large family of five children that helped him run his substantial farm needed to support the appetites of the large boardinghouse he operated.

Photograph circa 1918. Mrs. Augusta (Gussie) Deyo cutting children's hair at Howell's Half Orphan Home. Mrs. Deyo was the superintendent of the home.

October 1923.

Millions of invisible radio waves are passing through your home this very instant. They are loaded down with good things and are within your grasp. Are you going to do anything about it? See Mr. St. John about a radio set that will turn these wonderful waves into music and song, into instruction, recreation and happiness.

New Comston Park. Negative, circa 1915. At one time around 1845 this was the substantial farm of some 200 acres belonging to Austin Newcomb. In 1868 his son George purchased the farm. Geroge was very prosperous and decided he should get into the boardinghouse business just like the Osborns, the Thompsons and Mr. Davis across the road.

And so New Comston Park was born. It would become a large and extensive property with many buildings and amusements. For many years George hosted "The Farmers Picnic" at Newcomb's Grove. In 1897 over 3,000 people and nearly 500 wagons were in attendance.

In the early 1920s the property was bought by F.J. Khuen (phone number 54F2, if you care to make a reservation). Later it became the Olympia Hotel, which was eventually torn down. It is now the site of Crystal Pond Condominiums.

Old Union Society House. Picturesque Catskills, *1894. This was a very old landmark in Old Windham.*

Sometime around 1812, Major Fuller erected a house and tavern on the old turnpike (Old Road). When the new turnpike was laid out in 1826 and the old road was abandoned, Fuller built a new house and tavern just east of Davis's Pleasant Home. "Drover's taverns," as they were called, were located several miles apart across the mountaintop to service the many drovers of cattle and other farm animals, as well as teamsters transporting farm produce and manufactured goods to the port in Catskill. These taverns were a popular place for social gatherings and worship services before churches were built. Fuller's Tavern served as a post office for many years. Fuller's old tavern on Old Road became the home of William Pelham.

Fuller's Hotel continued for many years, later becoming the house and farm of Hezokia Rappleyea. Sometime around 1950 the hotel became a boardinghouse called Trails End, owned by Mrs. Hero until about 1960, when it was abandoned and eventually torn down.

Brook Lynne

About one mile east of Windham Village we come to the junction of the Windham Turnpike and the Brook Lynne Road heading south to Hensonville. The proximity of the turnpike and the Batavia Kill made for the establishment of many industries in the early days. In the short time frame of thirty years, there were tanneries, bark grinding mills, a distillery, an ashery, Camp and Lemily's woolen mill, sawmills, a carding mill, a cider mill and a shaving box factory. For the few farmers living nearby, all this activity, the constant squeal from ungreased pulleys and gears, earned the area the name "Old Fiddle" for several decades.

The Brook Lynne Bridge, built about 1896. Photograph circa 1900. This beautiful photograph, reminiscent of an iconic Currier and Ives print, typifies the charming beauty of Windham that attracted thousands of visitors to spend time in our little corner of paradise.

The bridge was one of the first iron truss bridges erected after a number of wooden ones were swept away. The large building in center is Soper's boardinghouse, The Pines. On the left is Soper's Bowling Alley.

Thankfully, by 1864, when John Soper obtained the old Harmon Camp house and factory, most of the other mills had closed or moved to other locations, making for a quiet and beautiful location to live. John filled out and enlarged the old house into a boardinghouse, ushering in a new era for Old Fiddle. Shortly after, Elbert Osborn bought the old Morss Farm and began what would become a very large family-run boardinghouse for over 100 years.

Elbert's good friend Ira Thompson from North Settlement, taking Elbert's advice that running a boardinghouse was easier work than farming the rocky soil of the Catskills, bought the old Reynolds place next to the Osborn House. This was the beginning of what would become a boardinghouse of distinction. The Thompson House, much expanded, is still operating today and is the last of the old hotels operating in the old boardinghouse tradition in Windham. Through dogged determination, diligence, hard work and a love for Windham and what they do, the Thompson family has pampered the summer, and now winter, visitors for 133 years and counting!

Why Brook Lynne? What best can be figured out is that one of those early visitors returned to the city and told their friends how much Old Fiddle looked like Brooklyn, New York City. The name has stuck until today, even the bridge being referred to as the Brook Lynne Bridge.

Old Mills. Glass plate, circa 1890. This vintage photograph is looking southeast over the Batavia Kill toward Brook Lynne. At the left is the old wooden Brook Lynne Bridge, the last of several wooden bridges to span the creek. Most bridges in the area were of the same style and construction. Upper right is Charles Soper's The Pines. The buildings lower right were used for the manufacture of shaving boxes by John Soper, with ornamental wood work added by his son Charles. Notice the dam below the bridge, in center, which diverted water to an overshot waterwheel.

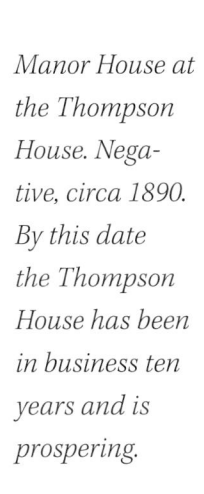

Manor House at the Thompson House. Negative, circa 1890. By this date the Thompson House has been in business ten years and is prospering.

Soper's "The Pines." Photograph circa 1940. It is hard to believe that this elegant establishment began as the simple small home of Harmon Camp. In 1864 Harmon sold his house to John Soper, who was already in the shaving box business several rods north of this house. The house was in poor condition, but Soper immediately began improvements. He made many additions over a twenty-year period, including adding more floors to the original edifice until it had reached the grand proportions shown in this picture. There was running water on every floor for the guests' convenience. There was a large observatory with a most charming view of the countryside.

When Soper first opened his boardinghouse, it was called The Evergreen Park House, after all of the evergreen trees around the house. In later years The Pines was purchased by Anita and Ferris Thompson, and then by John and Mickey Goettsche in 1958. Thus began a new chapter in the Thompson House history.

Photograph circa 1938. Soper's Brook Lynne Casino and Amusement Hall, Bowling Alley and Store was built in the mid-1920s. Charles Soper spared no expense in providing entertainment to please his many boarders. In 1967 this complex was torn down to make way for the new Thompson House main building and dining room.

Spruce Cottage. Negative, circa 1900. Built in 1893 by Herbert Thompson and Neil Brandow, this was advertised as, "Truly an architectural gem both inside and out." The Cottage in its earliest days served as the family living quarters and remained so for over sixty years. By the mid-1950s the house was completely renovated into guest rooms with private baths.

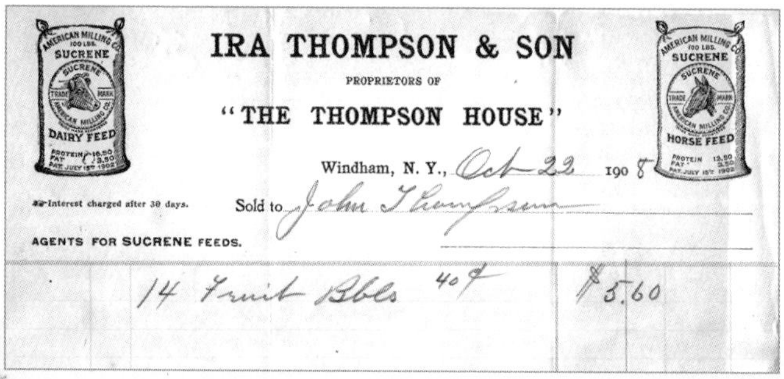

IRA THOMPSON & SON

PROPRIETORS OF

"THE THOMPSON HOUSE"

Windham, N. Y., Oct 22 1908

Interest charged after 30 days. Sold to John Thompson

AGENTS FOR SUCRENE FEEDS.

14 Fruit Bbls 40¢ $5.60

Photograph circa 1890. For many years the Sopers constructed dams on the west side of the Brook Lynne Bridge. Their purpose was to divert water to the different mills over the years, and also to flood the Batavia Kill upstream to allow for swimming and boating. Pity the poor gentleman trying to row a canoe with seven guests on board! That's the wooden Brook Lynne Bridge in the background.

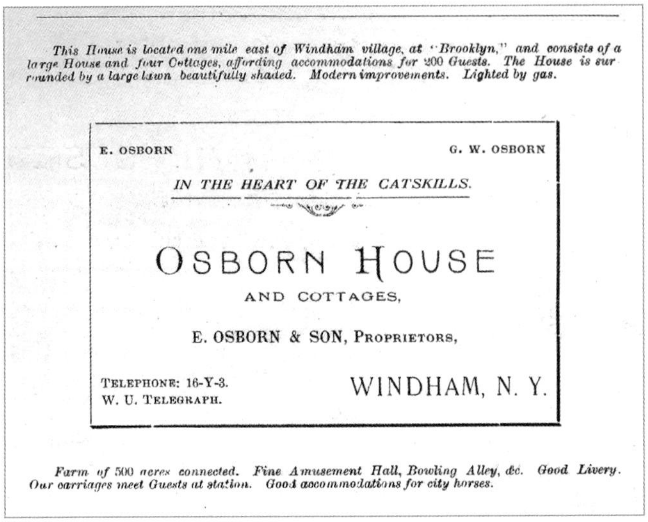
This House is located one mile east of Windham village, at "Brooklyn," and consists of a large House and four Cottages, affording accommodations for 200 Guests. The House is surrounded by a large lawn beautifully shaded. Modern improvements. Lighted by gas.

E. OSBORN G. W. OSBORN

IN THE HEART OF THE CATSKILLS.

OSBORN HOUSE

AND COTTAGES,

E. OSBORN & SON, PROPRIETORS,

TELEPHONE: 16-Y-3.
W. U. TELEGRAPH.

WINDHAM, N. Y.

Farm of 500 acres connected. Fine Amusement Hall, Bowling Alley, &c. Good Livery. Our carriages meet Guests at station. Good accommodations for city horses.

Elbert Osborn. Photograph circa 1885. Running a boardinghouse was much easier and more profitable than farming. It allowed for leisure time for Elbert to take his favorite horse and carriage for a ride in the countryside.

The Osborn House. Photograph circa 1895. In 1866 Elbert Osborn of North Settlement came down to Brook Lynne and purchased the old Morss farm and house. The buildings were careworn, and he began to make them like new, increasing the size of the main house. He immediately began taking in boarders, and thus the Osborn House was born. He also built two buildings to the left; the one pictured was Elbert's house, later called Cottage I. The other house was one he built for his son, George Osborn Sr. A house just north of these (Cottage III) was built for George's sister, Hilda Osborn Miller.

JANUARY 1864.

Mr. Harmon Camp has exchanged his residence and Broom Handle factory for the residence and Shaving Box Factory of Mr. John Soper. The former property was valued at $2,500 and the latter at $1,000.

The Osborn House. Photograph circa 1925. After many additions, the main house grew to hold 100 guests. Many people still remember the main house looking like it is pictured here.

A great number of Windham youngsters growing up, along with their parents, worked at one of the many large boardinghouses in Windham during the summer. I was lucky enough to work at the Osborn House in the late 1960s helping to cook three meals a day for the more than 200 guests. It was a wonderful experience for me, and I was treated very well by the families.

By 1946, after almost eighty years in business, the Osborn family sold the property to Walter Rubrecht, John Goos and Hans Jacobs. By the early 1970s it was inherited by Ken and Dottie Goos Stevens. (And who could forget Irene Rickard and Clarence Shufelt ["Shue"], who secretly ran the whole resort!) The Osborn House closed around 1974 when the main building was torn down.

Photograph circa 1940. George Osborn Jr. at the reception desk in the main house. The beauty of the wood paneling added to the charm of the hotel until the end of its days in 1974.

Photograph circa 1900. George Osborn Jr. giving rides to guests' children around the Osborn property. They are pictured in front of what was later to become Osborn's "Silver Casino."

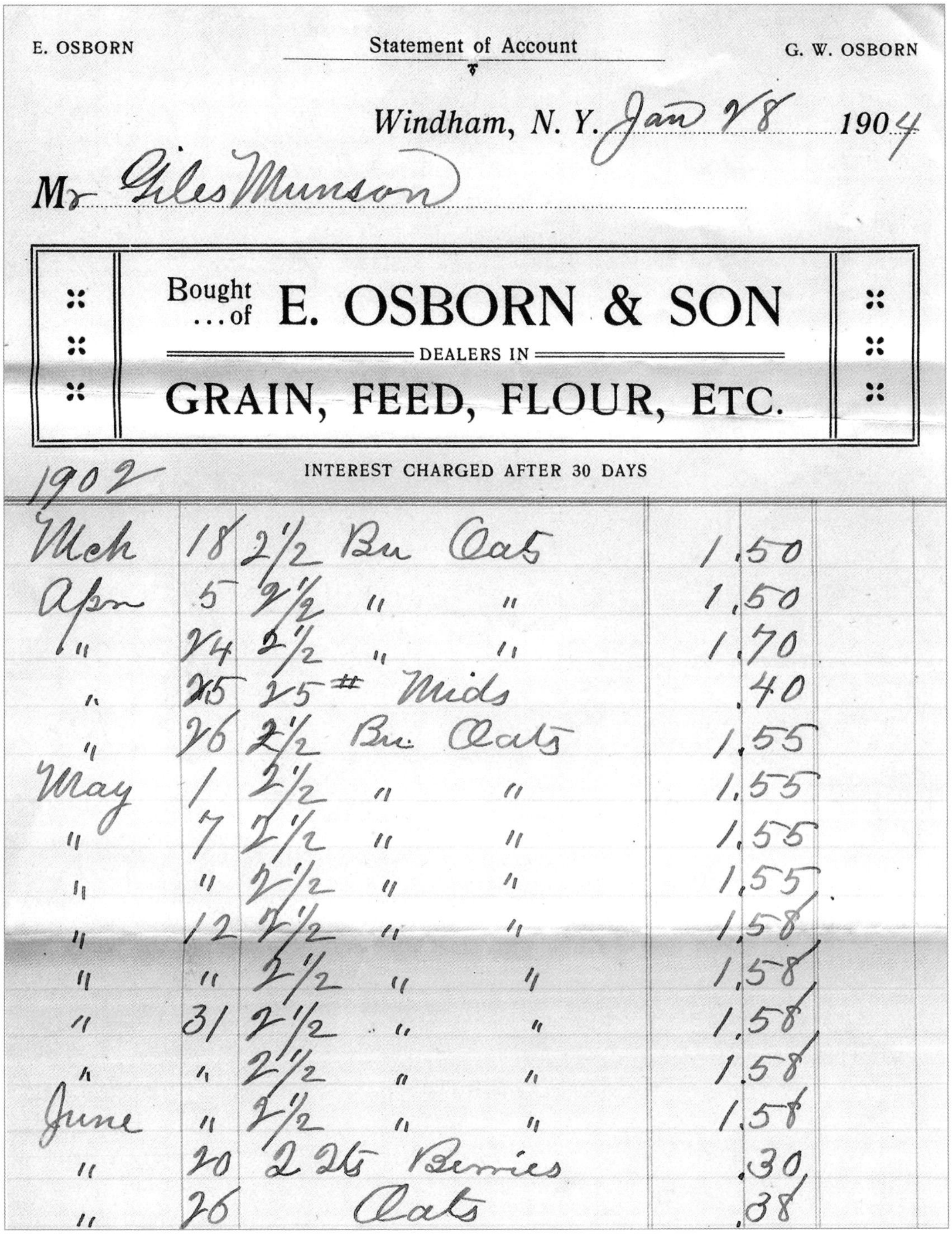

E. OSBORN | Statement of Account | G. W. OSBORN

Windham, N. Y. Jan 28 1904

Mr Giles Munson

Bought ...of E. OSBORN & SON

DEALERS IN

GRAIN, FEED, FLOUR, ETC.

INTEREST CHARGED AFTER 30 DAYS

1902

Mch	18	2 1/2 Bu Oats	1.50
Apr	5	2 1/2 " "	1.50
"	24	2 1/2 " "	1.70
"	25	25 # Mids	.40
"	26	2 1/2 Bu Oats	1.55
May	1	2 1/2 " "	1.55
"	7	2 1/2 " "	1.55
"	"	2 1/2 " "	1.55
"	12	2 1/2 " "	1.58
"	"	2 1/2 " "	1.58
"	31	2 1/2 " "	1.58
"	"	2 1/2 " "	1.58
June	"	2 1/2 " "	1.58
"	20	2 Qts Berries	.30
"	26	Oats	.38

June 1870.

Little girls who indulge in "jumping rope" should be very careful and not continue to exercise too long as our exchanges are already chronicling deaths in different sections from this cause. Careful parents will restrain their children.

January 1902.

W.J. Soper & F.J. Lacert have formed a co-partnership and will make Catskill mountain souvenirs and do a wholesale and retail business. It will be known as the Brook Lynne Novelty Works.

Water Sports on the Batavia. Photograph circa 1935. After many floods, the Soper dams were washed away. In 1931 George Osborn and the Thompsons agreed to build a new dam for their mutual benefit. A dam 76 feet long, 12 feet wide at the base and 8 feet high was erected. Thereafter the creek became quite deep, allowing for swimming, boating and high-diving acts. Into the mid-1960s, before there was a pool, no matter how tired we were, we only had to take a dip in the Batavia Kill to be shocked awake by the ice-cold water, even in July!

Hensonville

As we leave Brook Lynne and the Windham Turnpike, we continue south toward the small hamlet of Hensonville.

In the first thirty years in the settlement of Windham, the Windham-Hunter road was very rough and most likely one of those "roads less traveled." Hensonville was just a sharp bend in the road on one's way to Hunter. The Batavia Kill runs through Hensonville on its way to Windham Village. While narrow and usually not very strong, the stream still had potential for industry. We can only assume that John Henson and his family saw that potential to harness the stream to run mills when they decided to settle here in 1818 and built the first log house in the hamlet. Very shortly after, Ethan Bailey and his family came to Hensonville and built a house on the northwest corner of the four corners road, which gave the hamlet its original name—Bailey's Four Corners.

Postcard circa 1935. Sometime in the mid-1920s Claude and Bertha Mulford moved to Hensonville and purchased Hi-Ho Cottage, a small boardinghouse run by S. Colin. The renamed Maple Terrace began small, but expanded across the road with several buildings that had accommodation for 100 guests. The family business continued for over sixty years before closing. It became the private residence of Sheldon and Mary Warshow.

John Henson was a good man and a helpful neighbor. He built a sawmill and continued to help settlers build their homes and become a part of the community. In 1853 Henson was finally recognized with the changing of the hamlet name to Hensonville, and John Henson became the first postmaster. For over one hundred years Hensonville thrived with a surprising number of small businesses and boardinghouses for such a small community.

The Barnesdale. Postcard circa 1950. Erected in 1933 by Newman Barns, this was a fine-looking establishment with a lovely view from the rear of the house. After about twenty years the building was sold to Mr. Bourguignon, who renamed the boardinghouse Green Gables. By 1962 Richard and Patricia Pelham had bought Green Gables, upgraded it and ran a fine establishment. In later years it was called Bill Bailey's, The Silver Fawn and, lastly, Windhaven, before it burned and was torn down.

Hensonville United Methodist Church. Photograph circa 1890. The church was built in 1874 for about $4,400, with much labor provided by local families such as the Bloodgoods, Hayeses, Haneys, Chases, Griffins and others. The church flourished for many years as the Hensonville Charge, which combined the churches from Maplecrest and East Jewett with Hensonville.

By 1995, with dwindling membership, Hensonville merged with the Windham Ashland Community Church. Fortunately, both the Hensonville and Maplecrest church buildings have been saved and put to good use.

Donald and Edward Hayes at Ayres Fountain at the Junction of Route 296 and Brooksburg Road. Photograph circa 1910. To replace the old wooden watering trough in the middle of the road, George Ayres, a most devoted citizen of this community, erected a circular iron drinking fountain on Main Street for both horses and pedestrians. The horses were thankful for the fountain, but in later years it became an obstruction to cars and was removed. The bowl and pedestal now have an honored place in Hensonville Park on Main Street.

Main Street Looking South. Photograph circa 1906.

First building on right: Mr. Makely and Mr. McGlashan first operated their hardware store in this building around 1896. Later a new store was constructed farther south on Main Street. As early as 1922 Josef and Liesel Epping, both beauticians, owned and operated Josef's Beauty Mart here for over 50 years during the summers.

Other buildings right to left: The next small building is George Ayres Edison Shop. The next flat-roof building was Nelson Graham's Store. The sign in the window says "Boots, Shoes and Peanuts." Later on this was Pop Stoss's Pool Hall.

The house on the left was the early home of Ethan S. Bailey, the family from which the hamlet was first named "Bailey's Four Corners" in the early 1800s. The first post office in the hamlet was located here with Mr. Bailey as postmaster. After the Baileys passed on, the house was converted into a general store and meat market, at one time called Woodworth's Store. By the early 1920s Freda Blanche Decker purchased the premises and converted it back to a residence. It eventually became the home of Freddie and Barbara Decker.

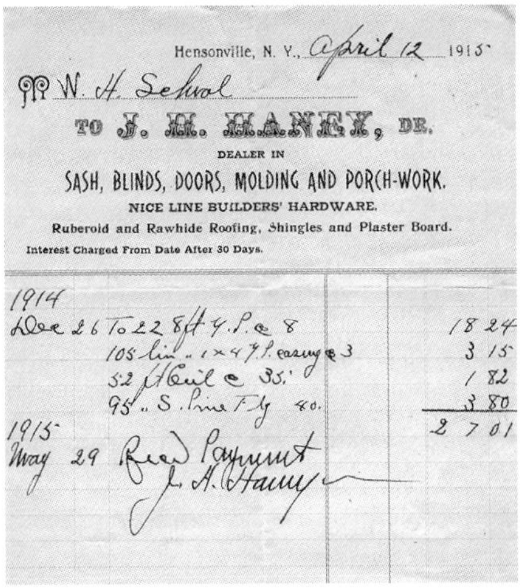

Hensonville, N. Y., April 12 1915

M W. H. School

TO J. H. HANEY, DR.

DEALER IN

SASH, BLINDS, DOORS, MOLDING AND PORCH-WORK.

NICE LINE BUILDERS' HARDWARE.

Ruberoid and Rawhide Roofing, Shingles and Plaster Board.

Interest Charged From Date After 30 Days.

1914		
Dec 26	To 22 8ft 4. P. @ 8	18 24
	105 lin. 1×4 P. casing @ 3	3 15
	52 ft Ceil @ 35	1 82
	95 " S. Pine F.g 40.	3 80
		27 01
1915		
May 29	Rec'd Payment J. H. Haney	

J.H. Haney Sash and Blind Shop. Photograph circa 1908. As early as 1881 Norris Cook opened a sash and blind business at this location. C.S. Lobdell was a wagon builder at this location as well. In later years J. Henry Haney took over the sash and blind shop. C.L. Jordan took over the blacksmith and wagon shop. The building collapsed during Tropical Storm Irene in 2011.

The Hensonville Post Office. Photograph circa 1900. As was the case in Windham Village, the post office in the Hensonville hamlet was located in several locations over the years, all because of politics. While very small, this building was much in demand, there being many enterprises located here at various times: Ray Vining's Barbershop; Miss Elizabeth Rouse's Green Parrot Gift Shop; and a Texaco gas station owned by Howard Drum, then John Dunbar, then Burt Wheat, who also ran a taxi service.

The Edison Shop. Photograph circa 1906. In this wonderful photograph we find Mr. Ayres at work in the little building he renovated to house his Edison Shop. Notice the phonographs in rear of the shop and the whole wall of recorded cylinders for sale. The object on the right is an early hand-cranked De Laval cream separator, which made the life of early farmers skimming the cream off the top of milk much easier. It was George's goal to improve peoples' lives.

Smalley's Theatre. Photograph circa 1950. In 1930 Horton Smith of the Hensonville Hotel wanted to keep one step ahead of neighboring village Windham. He and his friend Oscar Barker raised the money and built a large modern movie theater with a sloping floor and room for 300 people. Claude Soehl Jr. became the projectionist. The theater did well for many years. Mr. Smalley owned it for a time in the 1940s. The theater closed in 1955. The Town of Windham purchased the building and, with major renovations, it became Windham Town Hall. Ted Hoffman is sitting on the wall.

December 1925.

Clark J. Seeley with a force of men is making it possible for the Brook Lynne people who require a large quantity of ice for their use, to fill their ice houses in a jiffy, giving to his lately acquired up-to-date ice plow and equipment. Mr. Seeley purchased the ice on Cole's Glen Lake and is furnishing it to his patrons at a reasonable price per cake. Clark sure has the "pep."

Looking South along Route 296 in the Hamlet. Photograph circa 1905. Notice the old wooden watering trough provided for traveling animals. Behind the buggy on the corner of State Street (Brooksburg Road) is Griffin & Slater's dry goods store. It was built in 1861 by Mark Eggleston. This building was always a store and had several owners (Brockett & Parsons, The Brockett Bros., Laughran & Dedrick).

The large building next to the store is Griffin and Slater's storehouse with upstairs hall used for public events.

Griffin & Slater Store. Negative, circa 1905. After being a dry goods store for over eighty years, it became Muellars Bakery in the early 1950s. In more recent times it was the very popular eatery The Frog's House.

Orrin S. Griffen's "Rural Retreat." Photograph circa 1890. This is a large boardinghouse built by Mr. Merwin Griffen, who was a master carpenter. The retreat provided first-class accommodations for over forty years. In later years Orrin's daughter and son-in-law, Mr. and Mrs. Merritt McKean, and their daughter Leta took over the business and ran it for many years. A main attraction here was the two-story wooden "Summer House" (gazebo), where the Hensonville Band gave summer concerts. In the 1980s this was the home of Jim and Dottie Dunham.

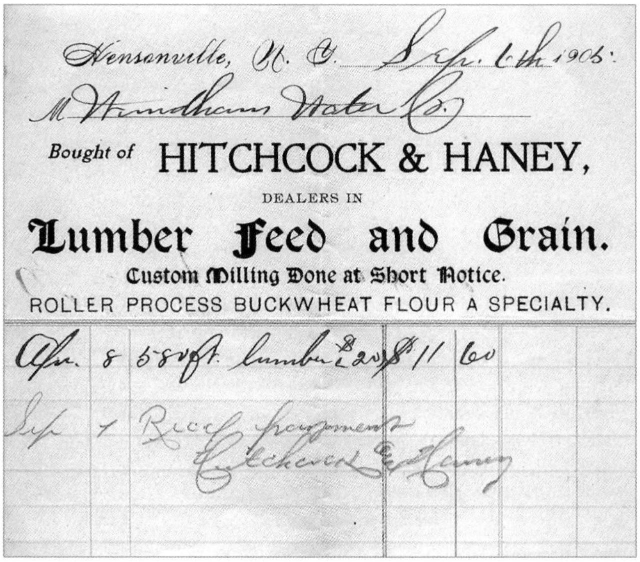
Hensonville, N. Y. Sep. 6th 1905

M Windham Water Co.

Bought of HITCHCOCK & HANEY,

DEALERS IN

Lumber Feed and Grain.

Custom Milling Done at Short Notice.

ROLLER PROCESS BUCKWHEAT FLOUR A SPECIALTY.

Hitchcock & Haney's Store on State Street. Postcard circa 1920. About 1884 William Hitchcock bought the existing house and grocery store. Ed Haney joined Hitchcock in later years, and together they built a dam in the Batavia Creek to create a channel of water to turn the waterwheel of his sawmill. A gristmill and grain store were added on later. This later became Mallory's ten-cent store.

JANUARY 1870.

The newly organized Morman Society will give on February 1st 1870, an oyster supper, at the Hotel of James Monroe. Mr. Miller, a disciple from Utah, will deliver a lecture on the subject of free-love; the profits will be used for the purpose of extending Mormonism. A general invitation is extended. The society now numbers 48 members. By order of the disciples of Hensonville.

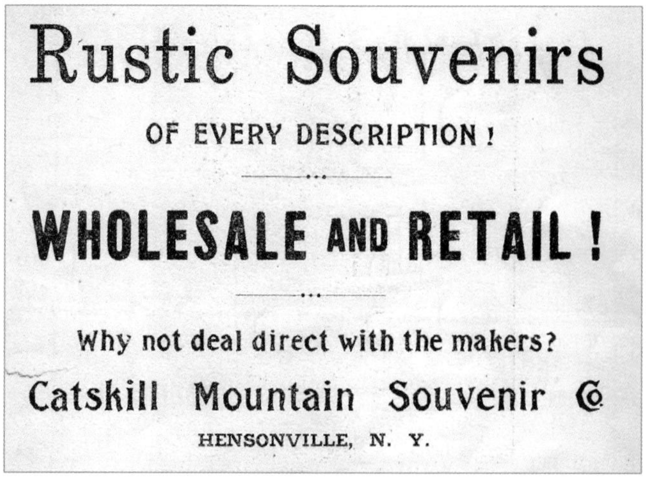

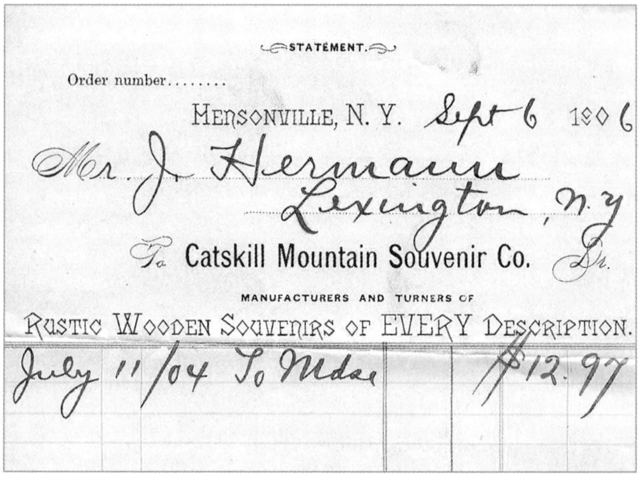
STATEMENT.
Order number........
Hensonville, N. Y. Sept 6 1906
Mr. J. Hermann
Lexington, N.Y.
To Catskill Mountain Souvenir Co. Dr.
MANUFACTURERS AND TURNERS OF
Rustic Wooden Souvenirs of EVERY Description.
July 11/04 To Mdse $12.97

The Chase House. Photograph circa 1920. The Chase family were early pioneers on the mountaintop. Zephaniah Chase and family settled in West Jewett around 1787.

Albert and Laura Woodworth Chase moved to Hensonville and built a large farmhouse circa 1845 and, along with their son Demont, they began taking in boarders. Demont's son Elbert Sr. took over the farm when Albert died. Elbert Sr.'s sister Leona took over running the boardinghouse for many years until she died and the business ended. The house was sold in the early 1970s.

Albert's great-great-grandchildren, Kevin and Christopher Chase, live near the old homestead today.

Harrison Beach. Photograph circa 1918. Harrison was born to John and Ann Drum Beach in 1844. By age thirty-one he met a young girl, age eighteen, with whom he fell in love. She soon gave birth to their first child, but died at childbirth. Two months later the newborn also died. Harrison was so overcome with grief that he could not recover. He immediately moved up onto the side of the mountain overlooking the village, where he lived the remainder of his 50-odd years, in grief for his wife and child. He became locally known as the "Hermit of the Catskills."

Janett Conley is on the right. This lovely poem by Elizabeth Rouse is in memory of Mr. Beach:

When night fall on the mountains
And the light is growing dim,
Can't you see a figure moving
Down the trail, that looks like him?
Can't you hear the tapping, tapping,
Of his stick among the stones
As he's coming with his lantern,
Coming down among your homes?
For the "Hermit of the Catskills,"
Though afar his soul may roam,
Every evening just at sunset
Comes to Hensonville, His Home.

MARCH 1887.

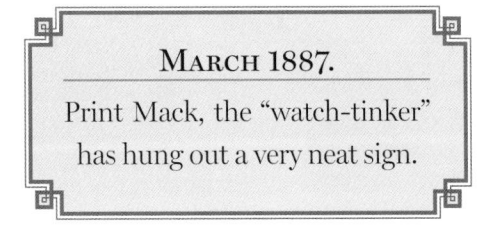

Print Mack, the "watch-tinker" has hung out a very neat sign.

Looking South along Upper Main Street. Photograph circa 1905. On the right side, at the corner of Main Street and Goshen Street, stands L.& I. Bloodgood's grocery store. Originally constructed as a boardinghouse in the mid-1800s by Mr. Rider, it was converted into a store in 1866, run by Brown and Laughran. The Bloodgood brothers took possession in the early 1880s. Their business did very well and expanded for over fifty years. The next structure up the road was a storehouse for the business. The Bloodgood brothers also ran a boardinghouse on Goshen Street that later became Spruce Manor. Today it is Vesuvio Restaurant.

Inside Levi and Isaac Bloodgood's Store. Photograph circa 1925.

JULY 4, 1884.
They are so temperate at Hensonville that they hardly put any lemon in their lemonade.

Hensonville Market. Photograph circa 1945. The former Bloodgood store was owned at this time by Walter and Ellie Jacobs.

Prohibition Convention. Photograph circa 1909. From 1795 through 1840, distilleries flourished on the mountaintop providing spirits to the many hotels and taverns along the main turnpikes. Driving cattle and hauling freight was a thirsty business.

But, somewhere along the line, after various religious denominations had become more established and churches had been built in every hamlet, issues of morality became more of a focus in the daily lives of families. The adverse effects of alcohol caused the Temperance Movement to take hold as well. Many new hotels, as well as already existing taverns, became temperance establishments, known as "cold water hotels." Up until the early 1970s some local boardinghouses were still labeled "dry establishments." This large gathering in Hensonville is most likely church-promoted.

DECEMBER 1903.

Stephen Pelham of this town won the gold watch prize at the Gilboa Xmas eve dance, as the best two-step dancer present.

Makely and McGlashan's Hardware Store. Photograph circa 1915. These gentlemen erected a new store south of Griffen's store around 1910 and served the community over a long period of time.

Photograph circa 1915. A rare picture of the inside of Makely and McGlashan's hardware store.

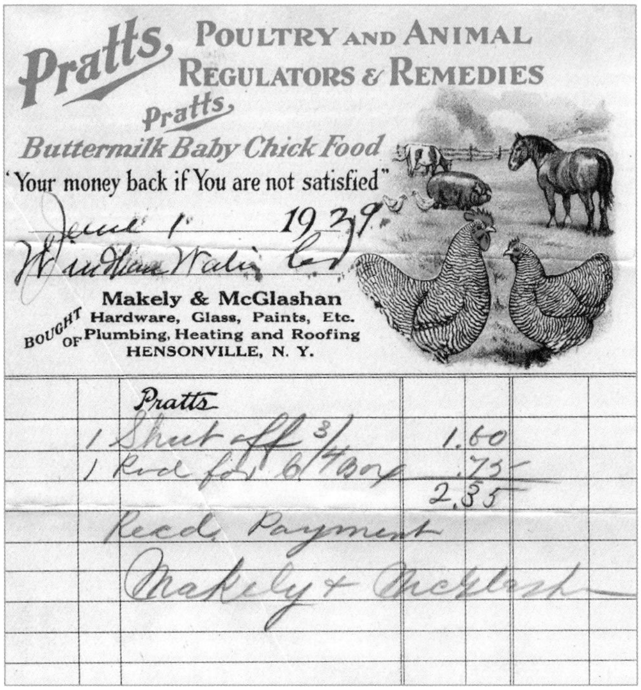

Pratts, POULTRY AND ANIMAL REGULATORS & REMEDIES

Pratts, Buttermilk Baby Chick Food

"Your money back if You are not satisfied"

June 1 1929

Windham Water Co

BOUGHT OF Makely & McGlashan
Hardware, Glass, Paints, Etc.
Plumbing, Heating and Roofing
HENSONVILLE, N. Y.

Pratts	
1 Shut off 3/	1.60
1 Rod for 6 ¼ Box	.75
	2.35

Recd. Payment
Makely + McGlashan

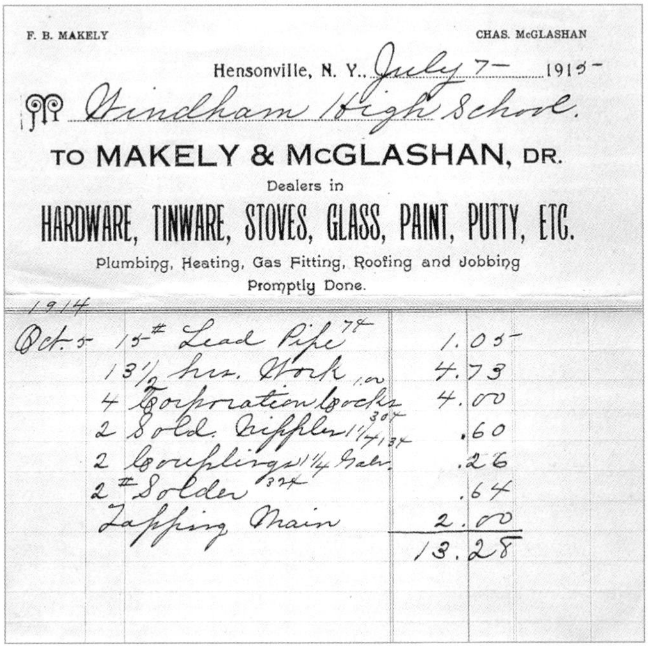

F. B. MAKELY CHAS. McGLASHAN

Hensonville, N. Y. July 7 1915

M Windham High School

TO MAKELY & McGLASHAN, DR.

Dealers in

HARDWARE, TINWARE, STOVES, GLASS, PAINT, PUTTY, ETC.

Plumbing, Heating, Gas Fitting, Roofing and Jobbing Promptly Done.

1914		
Oct. 5	15# Lead Pipe 7¢	1.05
	13½ hrs. Work 1.00	4.73
	4 Corporation Cocks	4.00
	2 Sold. Nipples 1¼ 30¢ 13¢	.60
	2 Couplings 1¼ Galv.	.26
	2# Solder 32¢	.64
	Tapping Main	2.00
		13.28

Looking North along Main Street. Glass plate, circa 1906. This clear and beautiful photograph was developed from a glass plate over one hundred years old.

On the right side is Griffen & Slater's store and storage building.

To the far left is George and John Winchell's meat market. The Winchell families were in Hensonville as early as 1867. Sometime after moving to Hensonville the two brothers opened their very profitable meat market. Theirs was a very clean and efficient store selling a few grocery items along with their meat, which they secured from animals raised by local farmers. They had a large ice box to preserve all of their perishables. This was later the site of Len Mallory's laundromat.

The little building next door was the Hensonville Hose Company. Then came Bloodgood's Store and storage building.

Hensonville Cornet Band. Photograph circa 1895. I'm not sure what the little building behind the band members was used for at this time. Perhaps it was for storage for Winchell Brothers, to the left. It later became the local firehouse.

While most villages on the mountaintop had a cornet band, even the small hamlet of Hensoville drew a large response when it formed its own. The gentleman to the left of the drum is Fred Makely, owner of the hardware store.

October 1946.

Does your "Gizmo" need repairing? Then bring it to Otto's Fix-It-Shop. Otto Goose, Hensonville.

Seeley's Ice Cream. Negative, circa 1935. George Seeley was another of Hensonville's very successful businessmen. At an early age he was already operating near the hamlet a large boardinghouse known as the Orchard Grove House.

George's eldest son, Clark, was also a hard-working and ambitious young man. Like his father, he struck out on his own and purchased the McGlashan house on Main Street, opening a small restaurant there. He liked the idea of having his own ice cream parlor, even though there were already many in the township. But, he decided, he would make the finest ice cream available, using a recipe given to him by his friend Roy Pelham. Seeley's Ice Cream was a major success, putting Hensonville on the map. He sold his product in bulk from Kingston to Albany for many years.

When the ice cream business declined, Clark's son Richard opened a bar here in spite of Prohibition. After Prohibition ended in the 1930s, the bar and restaurant became popular and successful. The Seeley family retired after three generations in business. They sold the restaurant and it became Martin & Sullivan's, another popular restaurant for several years.

Inside Seeley's Ice Cream Parlor and Restaurant. Photograph circa 1920. Serving customers are Evelyn Seeley Thetford and Alma Seeley. You can just make out postcards of the Catskill Mountain House on the rack.

Virginia's Lunch Room. Negative, circa 1946. Looking south along Route 296, Virginia Hough's new restaurant is in the former Winchell's Meat Market. Next door is the home of her parents, Mr. and Mrs. Elmer Hough. The building with the columns is today the post office. Notice the gas pump in front of the lunch room, just one of close to two dozen in the township of Windham. Today there are four gas stations in the township.

Gardinier and Maynard's Early Grist Mill. From Picturesque Catskills, *photograph circa 1884. Located just over the little bridge leading to Big Hollow, and nearly across from today's Gooss' Supermarket, John Gardinier and Spencer Maynard produced some of the finest grain in the county at their mill.*

1937.

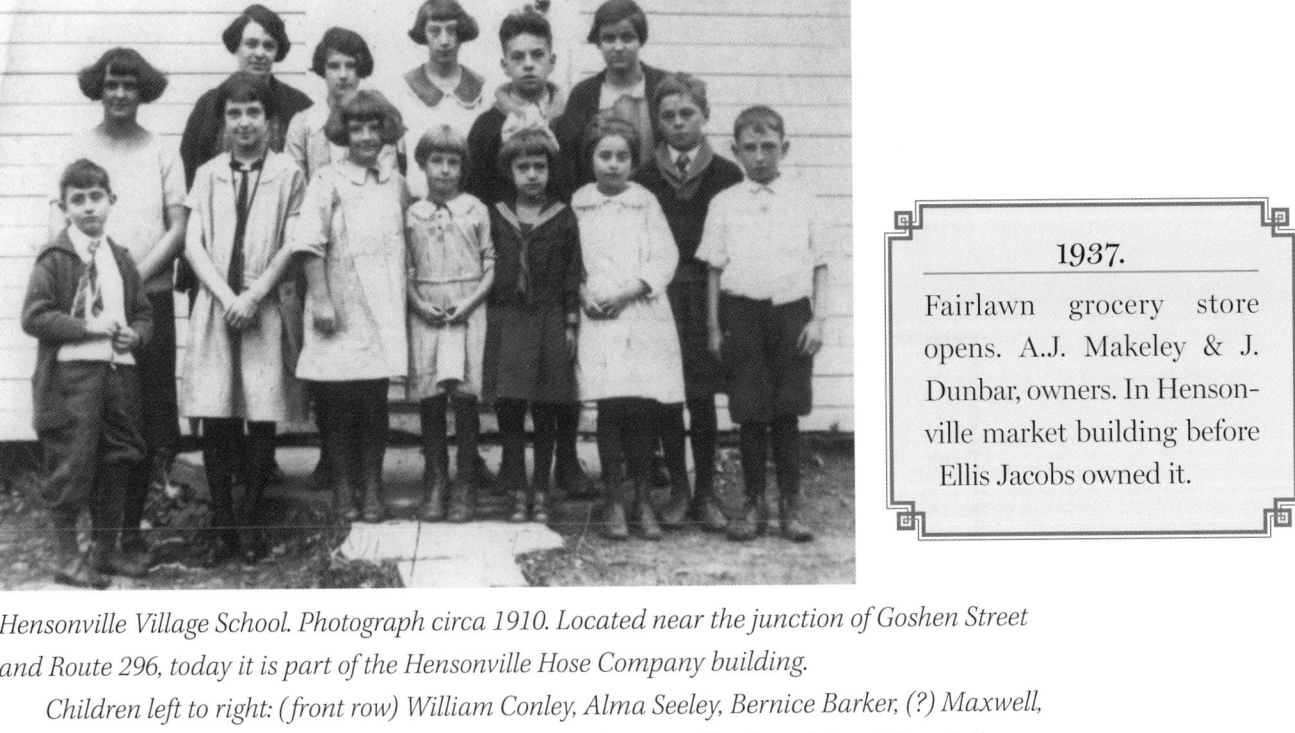

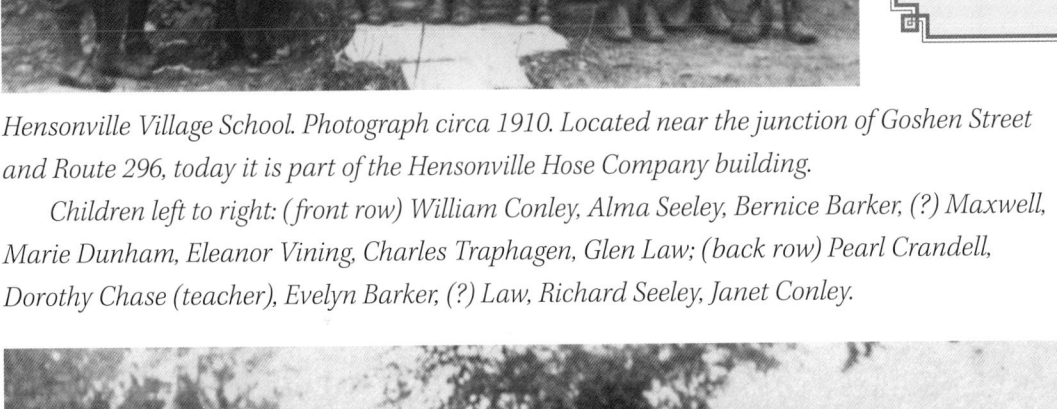

Fairlawn grocery store opens. A.J. Makeley & J. Dunbar, owners. In Hensonville market building before Ellis Jacobs owned it.

Hensonville Village School. Photograph circa 1910. Located near the junction of Goshen Street and Route 296, today it is part of the Hensonville Hose Company building.

Children left to right: (front row) William Conley, Alma Seeley, Bernice Barker, (?) Maxwell, Marie Dunham, Eleanor Vining, Charles Traphagen, Glen Law; (back row) Pearl Crandell, Dorothy Chase (teacher), Evelyn Barker, (?) Law, Richard Seeley, Janet Conley.

Road Crew. Photograph circa 1916. The state road crew of yesteryear, or is it today? It's hard to tell! Left to Right: John Winchell, William Pelham, Walter Pelham, Steven Pelham, Ted Osborn.

June 1905.

Hensonville citizens are determined that those lager beer wagons shall keep their beer out of this town.

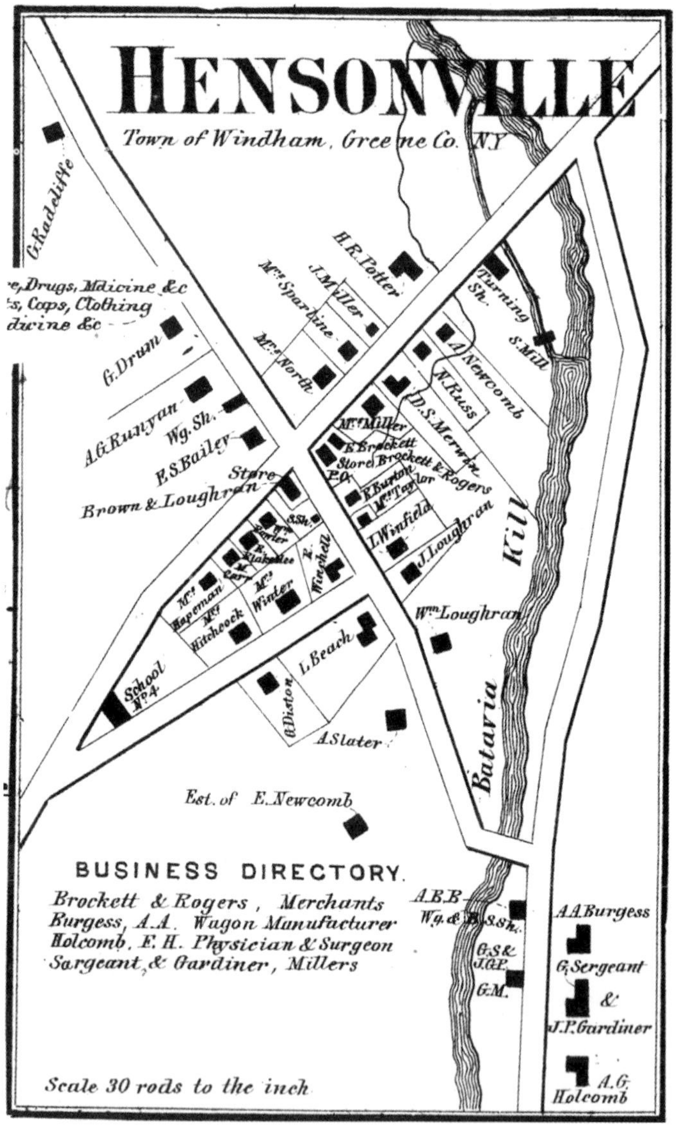

Big Hollow

Surely if ever there was a little piece of heaven here on earth, Big Hollow would be the place. Never destined for greatness, perhaps, it is nonetheless a magnificent fertile valley surrounded by the high peaks of the northern Catskills. When those early pioneers first arrived, they were awakened with an excitement to the possibility of a fresh new life. They were honest, decent, upright people of faith looking for a place of safety and serenity to do God's work for themselves and their neighbors.

And so it was that, in 1785, Deacon Lemuel Hitchcock and his family came to Big Hollow to start their new life. Word spread, leading other pioneer families like the Vinings, McGlashans, Barnums, Mosemans, DeLongs and many others to join this modest, hardworking community. Life was difficult at best in colonial times, but the land gave them almost everything they needed to sustain themselves.

Bridge and Post Office. Photograph circa 1928. Upon arriving at the hamlet of Maplecrest, we look across the Batavia Kill Creek toward Val Morrow's Fairview grocery store and post office. Notice the beautiful iron bridge that we pass over to enter the hamlet.

The Batavia Kill has its beginning here and, while small and tranquil except in spring or after heavy rainfall, it still provided the power for many mills. There were hemlocks for the tanners, hardwoods for the furniture makers, and the stone quarry for sidewalks, horse blocks, foundations, and for export to the cities farther south for paving and building.

Not unlike other areas of the mountaintop, what assured Big Hollow's future was its beauty and its ability to attract tourists to view what we have the privilege of living with every day. Most farm families had many children and soon had spare bedrooms. Their farmhouses became boardinghouses, attracting visitors to spend a week away from the heat and hassle of life in the big cities.

Sherwood Gus Moseman was one of the many taking on boarders at that time, and he realized the future possibilities for Big Hollow. He worked to have the name of the area changed from Big Hollow to Maplecrest to better reflect the beauty of the valley. By 1925 Gus began adding onto his house, and he continued to do so over a period of many years. Eventually he could accommodate over 500 guests, and the resort of Sugar Maples was born.

In 1960 Tom Meehan and Dick Vieth purchased Sugar Maples and operated it for another seventeen years, when it closed, thus ending another chapter in Big Hollow's history.

Today the peace and serenity of those early pioneer days has returned to this area.

To get a wonderful glimpse into life in this region in the late 1800s and early 1900s, one must read Elwood Hitchcock's books *Big Hollow* and *Hensonville.*

Village School District #4. Photograph circa 1915. The school was located on Maplecrest Road just north of Ron Garvey's Garage. Children left to right: (on bench) Alfred Rickard, Clara Winchell, Jessie Newcomb, Nellie Lary, Viola Vining, Gerald Newcomb; (middle row) Julia Law, Mildred Phelps, Claude Van Valkenburgh, Ethel Lewis, Leonard Vining, Ray Moseman (teacher), Walter Baker, Scott Vining, Alice Lewis; (back row) Lacy Crandell, Mabel Winchell, Sigsbee Van Valkenburgh, Bertha Winchell, Elmer Barnum, Crissie Hoyt, David Irish, Leon Van Valkenburgh, Elting Hoyt, Violet Newcomb.

Entering Maplecrest. Photograph circa 1942. From the village schoolhouse looking toward the hamlet, we see Robert Peck's garage on the left, which he built in the mid-1930s. On the right, until about 1920, was the Breakstone and Levine separating station where the farmers' milk was weighed and tested for butter fat and then the cream was separated from the milk. The cream was brought to the Windham Creamery and made into butter and, as time permitted, cheese. Raymond Woodworth and George Richard ran the creamery.

Robert Peck repaired cars and sold gas for many years before selling his business in 1943 to Ed Garvey and Ned Hitchcock. Garvey's son Ronald took over the business in later years; Ronald was an excellent mechanic in these parts. Both the garage and the old creamery were swept away in Tropical Storm Irene in 2011.

Morrow's General Store and Post Office. Photograph circa 1929. This very old structure was almost always a store. In 1829 it also became the first post office in the hamlet, with Friend Holcomb as postmaster. The store was the focal point in the community where you could learn the comings and goings of everyone in town. About 1850 William Henry Moseman became part-owner of the store and completely rebuilt it. He, along with Sherwood Gus Moseman, operated the store for nearly 75 years. Then, from 1925 until 1965, Valentine Morrow and his wife Irene ran the store while he also served as postmaster. A nicer or more accommodating man would be hard to find.

Shelter Rock. Photograph circa 1900. After crossing the bridge into Big Hollow, we take the road to the right and head up Maplecrest Mountain Road. As you pass through the second right-angle turn, on your left will be Shelter Rock. This very large overhanging rock—large enough to park a carriage under—has always been a point of interest for locals and visitors.

Photograph circa 1895. The Barnum family were early pioneers on the mountaintop. They first arrived circa 1810 and lived at various times in Lexington, Prattsville and, by 1868, in Big Hollow. Bethuel Barnum and Phoebe, his first wife, settled at the upper end of Rutland Road. They had nine children. Bethuel's second wife was Mary Magdalene Bunt, and she and Bethuel had another eight children. This has made for very large family reunions, even today!

The house pictured is Bethuel's son Martin's homestead on Barnum Road in lower Big Hollow. In later years Martin's brother Elmer raised his family here also. These were simple times, and Martin and his wife Carrie raised four children in this small home.

Reuben DeLong House. Photograph circa 1895. Along the Barnum Road we come across a neighbor of Martin Barnum named Reuben DeLong. Reuben and his wife Lydia Tompkins DeLong raised a fine family of nine children on this small farm.

January 1920.

What cannot be done under dry law; to buy or sell a drink anywhere except for sacramental or medicinal purposes; to give or take a drink anywhere except in the home of the man who owns it; to keep any liquor in storage anywhere but in your own home; to try to get such reserves out of storage, to carry a pocket flask; to have more than two drinking residences: one in the country and one in the city; to restock your home supply when it runs out; to manufacture anything above one half of one percent in your home; to move your home supply from one house to another without obtaining a permit, to get this you must prove that you came by the supply before July 1, 1919; to display any liquor signs or advertisements on your premises; to buy, sell or use a home still or any other devise for making liquor in the home; to buy or sell any formulas or recipes for homemade liquor; to make a present of a bottle of liquor to a friend; to receive such a present from a friend.

Blacksmith Shop. Photograph circa 1910. Across the road from the village post office stood the local blacksmith shop of Mose Hitchcock. His location between the post office and Sugar Maples made his place a social Mecca in his later years. He loved to converse with tourists. In the late 1920s the blacksmith shop became more of a curiosity to city folk than a working shop, because the automobile had taken over the streets.

The little boy with Mose in the picture is Elwood Morrow.

October 1870.

If sufficient cider is poured into a barrel so that it will run from the bung, when fermentation commences, a large quantity of vermin, resembling those found in apples, will be thrown out by the foaming cider. People frequently allow cider when it is intended to be used as a beverage, to remain in a closely plugged barrel or cask, and thereby the vermin are retained in the cider which undoubtedly gives it a decidedly rich flavor.

A Fine Gentleman. Photograph circa 1910. Mose Hitchcock, the village blacksmith. His small shop was built by Ambrose Hadden many years before 1910.

Main Street before Sugar Maples. Photograph circa 1915. Looking east, the corner of the house on the right is Mose Hitchcock's home. The second house is that of John Moseman and, later, Ray Moseman. The next house is that of Romaine Law. This house was bought by Sherwood (Gus) Moseman and John Martin. They renovated the house and it became the first Sugar Maples in 1925. The fourth house belonged to Walter Bray. The building far left is the Dorland and Allen Moss house.

Looking East along Main Street after Sugar Maples Was Built. Postcard circa 1940. The Methodist Church on the right owes its beginnings to Bethuel Barnum and his family. The church building was erected in 1857 and served the residents of Big Hollow for fifty years before joining the churches of Hensonville and East Jewett and becoming the Hensonville Charge. At that time there was one pastor for three churches. With declining membership, the church closed its doors in the 1980s.

Photograph circa 1903. Here is a wonderful picture of the Irish Boys. These three young men—David, George and Lewis Irish—were the sons of John and Josephine Irish. They lived in a house up the Mountain Road behind the post office. John was a cobbler by trade, but also made and repaired harnesses.

David Irish, father of Doris Irish Garvey of East Jewett, was the caretaker for Sugar Maples for very many years. George Irish, father of Lois Irish Jenkins of Lexington, was a master carpenter. Lewis Irish became a farmer, but died very young in what I believe was a farming accident.

October 21, 1928.

Maplecrest was visited on Sunday by no less a personage than Miss Helen Keller who is internationally known. Miss Keller was accompanied by Mrs. Macy of Onteora Park. They were calling on Mrs. Albert Ising. Although unable to see, hear or speak, Miss Keller made known the names and colors of flowers simply by the sense of touch. She also remarked that the scenery here was wonderful. We understand she has written a book which is soon to make its appearance.

Maplecrest Baseball Team. Photograph circa 1927. Baseball was not only a major pastime in school, it was an important pastime for adults as well. Every town, village and hamlet had organized baseball games, and the competition between local teams was fierce. The Maplecrest ball team consisted of the following gentlemen, left to right: (front row) Elwood Hitchcock, Gerald Moseman, Ralph Barnum, Paul Tompkins, Paul Joyce, Charles Traphagen, Wilfred Hitchcock (sitting on ground); (back row) Lawrence Peck, Burdett Woodworth, Sheldon Peck, Walter Baker, Floyd Christian.

Big Hollow Presbyterian Church. Photograph circa 1920. In 1822, twenty-one settlers in the hollow formed the Presbyterian Church Society. Two small meetinghouses were built early on. With the congregation growing larger, a new and larger church, as pictured, was built in 1854. The church flourished for nearly another hundred years before it was deeded over to the Free Methodist Society in 1948. The Free Methodist Church still flourishes today with a strong bond among the descendents of the early settlers.

Harold and Donald Baker. Photograph circa 1945. The family dog had puppies, to the great delight of Don and Harold. The boys were two of the five children of Walter and Dorothy Vining Baker. Walter was an avid hunter and operated a black fox breeding farm for a time before working for the NYS Conservation Department as an animal control officer. His son Donald was for many years the pastor of the Maplecrest Free Methodist Church. Harold operated a John Deere lawn mower and snowmobile dealership in Hensonville.

May 1870.

The tiniest thing in nature was made for a purpose. Even the fly who has been "shooed" almost to death, has at least one mission to fill. He keeps bald-headed sinners awake at church, on a warm day, so that their unregenerated hearts may be touched by the words of the minister.

Platt Hitchcock Family. Photograph circa 1890. Hitchcock is a very old and respected name in the history of Old Windham. In 1795 Deacon Lemuel Hitchcock, grandfather of Platt Hitchcock, became the first settler in this area of Windham called "Big Hollow." Platt and his wife Emerett settled on a small farm just east of the hamlet around 1856. They raised five children in a little red farmhouse. Platt's brother Dwight built the present-day large white farmhouse in 1900. Platt's son William and his wife Grace Crandell raised their family in the new house. The tradition of raising fine large families continues to this day.

Left to right: (front) Emerett at age 54, her sister Earania, age 58; (rear) Platt, age 58, Dwight, age 16, Rose, age 25, William (father of Wilfred Hitchcock).

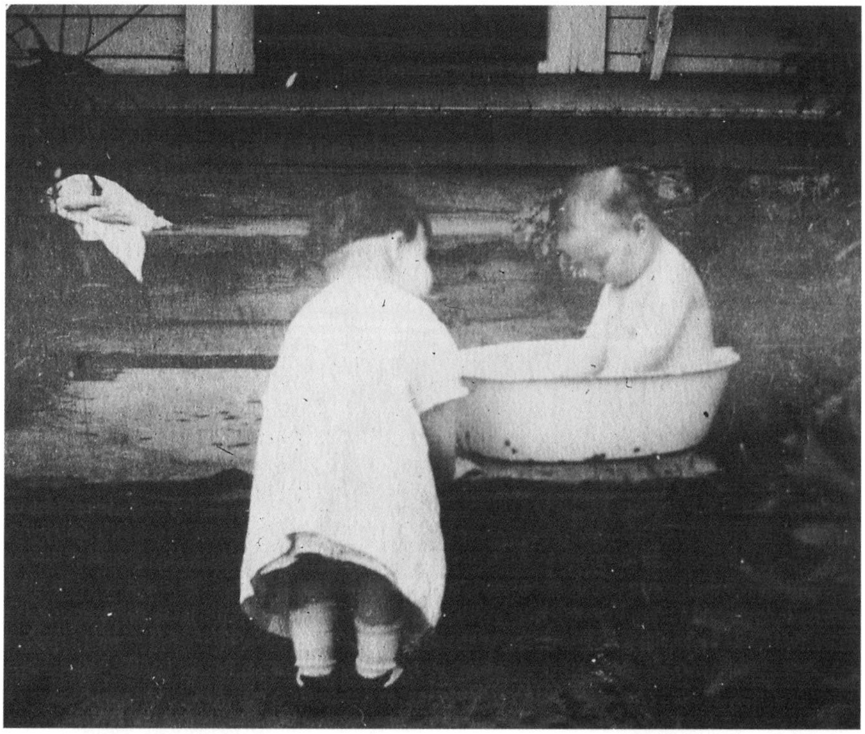

Photograph circa 1920.
This wonderful photograph circa 1920 needs very little explanation. We find Wilfred Hitchcock, maybe one and a half years old, on the front steps of the old farmhouse taking his regular bath. I'm sure his friend Emma Planck is making sure he washes in all the right places.

Jacob Planck House. Photograph circa 1910. Planck's farm was located at the top of the hill above William Hitchcock's farm. Lou Martin and son Tom's Wild West Town was located here in the mid-1950s. The ranch offered horseback riding, amusement rides and miniature golf. It operated until around 1960. The people on the porch are, left to right: Mrs. Campbell, Maud (?), John Planck and Rover, Mr. Inetzke and dog Jack, Rose Delong,. Mr. and Mrs. Jacob Planck.

Photograph circa 1915. The great hunters over in East Jewett had nothing on the local boys in Big Hollow! Allen Moss, Ray Osborn and Howard Crandell with coons at Howard's home.

Austin Hitchcock House. Photograph circa 1907. Sometime around 1930 Austin took over his father Zalmon's farm, just below the present-day flood control dam. Zalmon ran a small but very productive farm. His parents at one time took in summer boarders. Austin didn't have the heart for farming, but loved mechanical work and worked for a time in Robert Peck's garage. He had found his professional calling and later moved to Kingston to pursue his trade.

This house has been faithfully restored and is owned by Tom and Mary Donovan.

Batavia Manor House. Postcard circa 1920. About halfway down Big Hollow Road we come to the junction with Peck Road, which heads mostly northerly toward East Windham. We pass Newell Peck's farm, then Howard Crandell's farm, and then come to a sharp right turn in the road. This is the site of Newcomb Chatfield's farm and boardinghouse.

Newcomb and Grace raised two children here who attended the one-room schoolhouse across the road. Newcomb taught school here in 1890. There were three schools in Big Hollow in the mid- to late 1800s. The Peck Road School was moved to Rutland Road around the turn of the century, and the Upper Big Hollow School District #2 was closed.

This is the present home of Bernard and Lisa Chen, who have faithfully restored the home to its former glory.

Jabez Barnum Farm. Photograph circa 1905. This is one of three farms in Big Hollow that Jabez owned in his lifetime. The farm pictured is located at the junction of Big Hollow Road and Peck Road. The house is still there. In recent times it was the home of Mr. Cola Batista.

When Jabez and his wife Elizabeth Bray first moved to Big Hollow, they settled on a farm just east of the house in this picture. Not unlike other farmers in the area, Jabez enlarged the house to accommodate several boarders, adding to the family income. Jabez also became a skilled mason, erecting chimneys and doing concrete work. In his spare time he became an accomplished musician, teaching his four sons to play instruments and organizing the Barnum Band, which played at social functions.

September 1895.

There has been quite an improvement in our village since 1875. There was no store, and mails only twice a week. Now we have daily mail, a store, and steam sawmill, ten new residences and nearly all the old ones repaired, also a paper in circulation for raising funds for a sidewalk on one side of the road and streetlamps are being talked of. "Isn't Big Hollow booming?"

Jabez Barnum Family. Photograph circa 1908. Taking a break from the many farm chores to pose for this family portrait, we find, left to right: (front) Elizabeth Barnum, Julia Barnum, age four, Ralph Barnum, age six, Jabez Barnum; (rear) Olin Barnum, age thirteen, Fanny Barnum, age fourteen, Walter Barnum, age twenty, Will Barnum, age eleven.

George Ruland. Photograph circa 1900. In this wonderful picture we find George Ruland churning butter, one of those necessary chores done at every homestead. George and his wife Hattie Irish were not blessed with children, but were very self-sufficient in operating their small farm. About the turn of the century, the Upper Big Hollow School District #2 was closed and the Peck Road School was moved to George's property, becoming the new upper school on Ruland Road.

The Elmhurst. Photograph circa 1936. We are now at what was the earlier home and boardinghouse of Jabez Barnum. By 1930 the farm was sold to George Irish and his wife Julia Barnum. They named their place The Elmhurst and operated the boardinghouse for about eighteen years. The pretty little girl in the wagon is Lois Irish Jenkins, six years old.

Upper Big Hollow Schoolhouse on Ruland Road. Photograph circa 1908.

Left to right: (front row) Willis Chatfield, Robert Newcomb, Mildred West Southerland (teacher), Ralph Barnum, Nick West; (middle row) Robert Peck, Charles West, Louise Chatfield, Fanny Barnum, Cecil Crandell, Bessie Peck; (back row) Olin Barnum, Harry Briggs, Will Barnum, Daisy Newcomb, Laura West, Lucy Crandell, Julia Barnum.

Leon McGlashan Farm. Photograph circa 1930. This is one of two McGlashan homesteads in Maplecrest. George and Lola McGlashan moved from South Jewett to Maplecrest in the mid-1920s, operating a small farm, boardinghouse and sugar house. Leon followed in his parents' footsteps. His method of producing maple syrup was a classic operation using buckets and horse and sleigh to collect sap. The Museum of Natural History in New York City was so impressed with Leon's operation of syrup making that they commissioned a diorama of it to be made and displayed for the public to see. It's still on display today.

A distant relative and earlier settler of Big Hollow was John McGlashan. His grandson Leroy was an engineer on the Catskill-Cairo Railroad for a number of years, then ran the McGlashan Homestead Farm after he married. For thirty years Leroy was the chief engineer on the Otis Elevated Railroad. His son Milton, a skilled carpenter, operated the farm and a large maple syrup business for many years.

November 1900

P.O. Hitchcock has running water to his house, barn and trough by the roadside. Reuben Delong laid the logs.

Martha West and Family. Photograph circa 1920. Farther up the valley is the Adelbert and Martha West farm. Shortly after fathering six handsome children with Martha, Adelbert took ill and died suddenly. He left Martha with the daunting task of raising six children on a small farm. Martha rose to the task and, with love and a dogged determination, instilled a work ethic that enabled the children to help with the family's needs and expenses. The house is still standing today, and West family members are still living in Maplecrest.

Left to right: (front) Leon, born 1906, Laura, born 1898, Lena, born 1906, Martha, Lester, born 1903; (rear) Nicholas, born 1901, Betty West Rhoades's grandfather, Charles, born 1896. Three children died young—Sherwood, Floyd and Mable.

Walter Barnum. Photograph circa 1930. For Walter it was not bad enough that he had to take a bath, outdoors no less, but obviously with very little privacy! Walter is about ten years old here. He was the son of William Barnum and grandson of Jabez Barnum.

Martha West and Son Leon. Photograph circa 1918. Martha, with six children to feed, probably spent much time with the butter churn. Her son Leon is waiting to take his turn. Leon was born deaf and dumb. Despite the hardships of raising six children on her own, Martha still managed to send Leon to the Batavia, New York School for the Deaf.

Photograph circa 1910. Two more first-class hunters in Big Hollow— Maurice Planck and Irving Mallory with a fine haul of coon skins.

August 1907.

A Big Hollow horse was so frightened by an auto in this village [Windham], that it came near dying after going home. It lay down, overcome and veterinary Turk had to be called. What a pity it is that the State did not own separate roads for the autoists, and others for the horses. There are people in town who own horses that cannot overcome the animal's fear of the gas machines and the animals are practically worthless.

Photograph circa 1915. Another young hunter—Robert Newcomb with a bobcat he shot.

Photograph circa 1940. We are now three-quarters of the way up the Big Hollow valley and we have arrived at the home of Ebbie and Pearl Newcomb. Visiting Pearl and Ebbie is their daughter Beulah Newcomb Strausser and her children Robert, Harvey, Donald and Gloria. Beulah and her brothers Jay and Robert were born and raised at the very far end of the valley, opposite the Gundersen family. The house is long gone. Beulah's husband was Ken Strausser, a master carpenter whom I had the pleasure to learn from and work with in the late 1960s.

Many years later Ebbie moved down the valley to the little building pictured. In the mid- to late 1800s, this was the Upper School District #2. Leon McGlashan's father George went to school here, and Newcomb Chatfield was the teacher.

Photograph circa 1910. Jerome Crandell operates his portable sawmill, using a Hit and Miss gas-powered engine, somewhere in the Big Hollow valley. Jerome moved his mill from site to site, cutting lumber for new houses and for the furniture making industry. The sawyers are, left to right: Jerome Crandell, Howard Crandell, Gene Mallory, Frank Hanley, Irving Mallory, Manly Mallory.

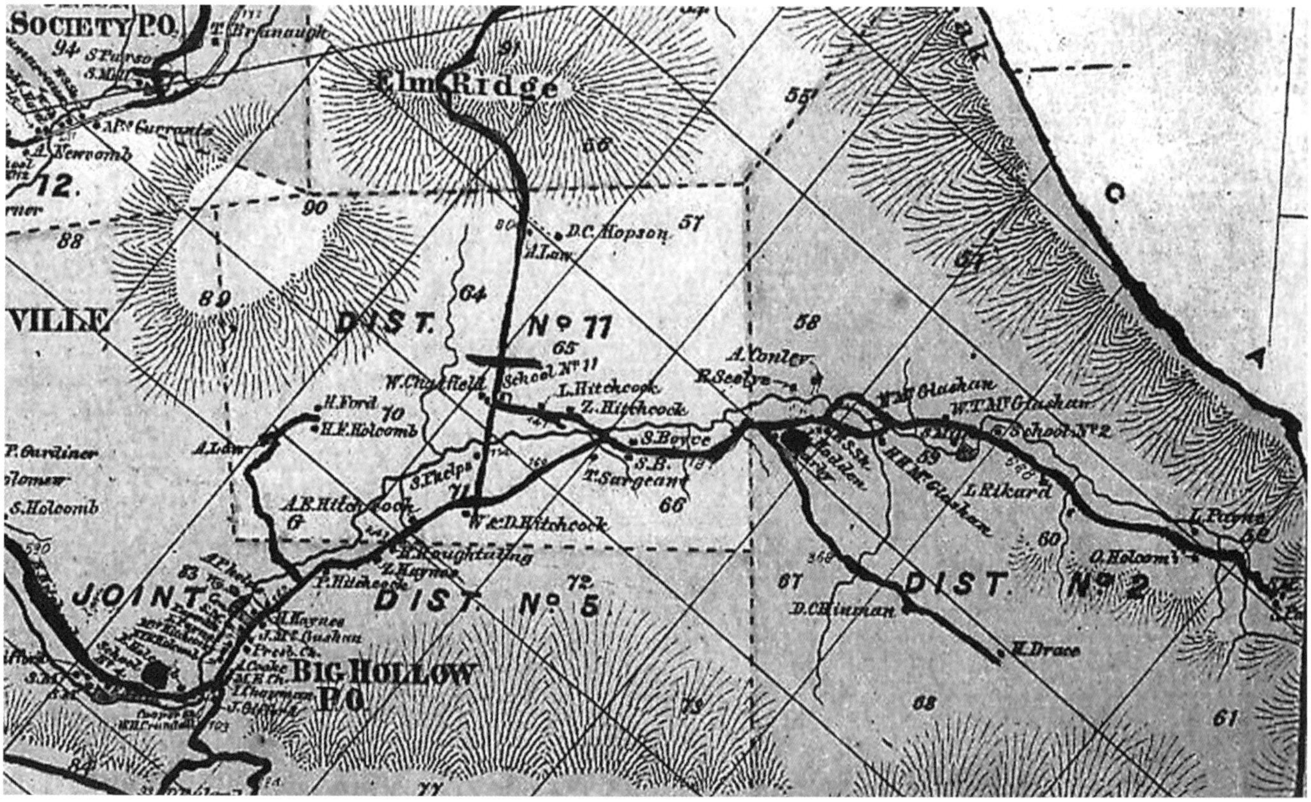

Big Hollow Map 1867.

Windham Village

This beautiful panoramic view of Windham Village circa 1890 speaks well of a thriving community. The first thing one might notice is the lack of trees. All of the hemlock trees have been cut down for their bark and used in the tanning process. The hardwoods that are left are still being harvested for furniture making, farm implements, brooms, shaving boxes, trim work in houses, etc. Many of the hemlock trees, after the bark was removed, were used to build homes and businesses.

It's 1890, and the mountaintop is now a major tourist destination. City folk flock to Windham to enjoy its scenic beauty, fresh air and wholesome fresh food, and simply to rest and relax. The land around the village has been taken over by the dairy industry. There is much pasture land for the thousands of cows providing milk and butter and cheese for the visitors to the mountains. So much was produced, in fact, that milk was shipped off the mountain to the cities to the south.

The Mohican Trail passes through the fairly densely populated village of homes and businesses that provided most of the necessities of life. At least two of every trade could be found along Main Street. Businesses were bought and sold, and partnerships changed with such frequency that exact dates of ownership of a particular business are hard to establish. This illustrates how easily early businesses were able to adapt to changing market conditions and the needs of the consumer simply by changing from one trade or enterprise to another. Businesses also changed

Windham Village Panorama. Photograph circa 1895. We are looking north over Windham Village from South Mountain. The Windham Centre Church/Civic Center is in the lower left, center, with the Methodist Church right, center. The house, bottom center, is the Silas Munson House. Today it's the Durnan house at the top of Church and South Streets. South Street runs across the bottom of the photo with the old Munson house on the right. The large house, center, just above Main Street, is the old Glen House. In modern times it was the Lublie house and then Roger Mulley's residence.

location at will. Owners were always looking for some retail advantage at a new location. If they liked their building, but not the location, they just picked up their shop and moved it to a more desirable location with hardly a second thought.

As you look at the following photographs, you will notice the great pride our ancestors took in the way their village looked and how that would represent them to the world that passed through or came to visit. Also evident is the love they had for the land they worked and in sharing this area's beauty with appreciative visitors.

Today the pervasive industries that once dominated Main Street are gone. Sitting on the front porch at the nearest boardinghouse is almost a thing of the past. Today's visitors to Windham are on the go. In the summer they come to hike, bike, fish, hunt wildlife, camp and savor what nature has to offer. In the winter they come for skiing and snowmobiling. Today's businesses center on servicing tourists, which keeps Windham and the mountaintop prospering.

Approaching Windham Village from the East. Photograph circa 1905. We are looking down Creamery Hill with the Methodist Church steeple visible. On the right is the junction with Mitchell Hollow Road. A very early schoolhouse occupied the northwest corner, then the property of D.C. Tibbals.

The Elgin Creamery. Photograph circa 1915. Few creameries existed before 1875 on the mountaintop because most farms were small with few cows. Butter and cheese were homemade. This creamery was built in 1889 as the Catskill Mountain Creamery. In the late 19th century, as boardinghouses numbered in the hundreds and city populations grew, so did the demand for milk products. With the coming of the railroad and the improvements in the roads, the market opened up for the mountaintop farmers, and a flourishing dairy industry ensued. The little boy on the wagon is Irving Steele.

November 1868.

Messrs. George Baldwin, Truman Johnson, and Albin E. West have just opened a saloon, in the tin shop reeently occupied by S.D. Kingsley, for the sale of Confectionery, Oysters and Cigars. Greenbacks will be accepted as "legal tender" in payment of any of their commodities.

Kissock & Coons Monument Shop. Photograph circa 1895. Mr. Kissock was in business many years in various locations around Windham. This location is just east of the Methodist Church. At one time this was the residence and cooper shop of C. Watson Brigs (1875).

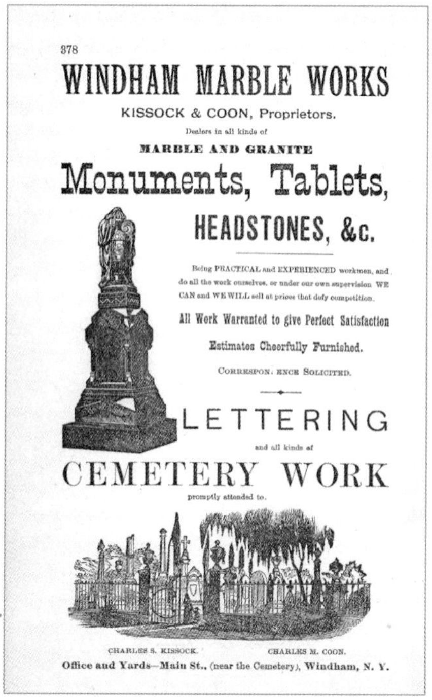

The Windham Methodist Episcopal Church, built in 1843. Photograph circa 1920. The society existed for about forty years previously and worshipped for a time in the Tibbals Schoolhouse on Mitchell Hollow Road. The Methodist Church and the Centre Presbyterian Church joined in 1970 to become the Windham Community Church.

The Merritt Osborn and Son Hotel. Photograph circa 1895. Located just west of the Methodist Church, this was one of the finest and most "proper" (temperance) hotels in Windham. A large building was attached to the rear of the hotel and was called Gothic Hall. The hall was used as a ballroom, but also for political purposes and other public meetings, socials and concerts. It was a very popular place for the more refined and cultured citizens of Windham and its surroundings. Circa 1865, Gothic Hall was removed from the hotel and moved west along Main Street. The hotel was later sold to the Methodist Church for use as a parsonage.

Looking East along Main Street from Mad Brook Bridge. Photograph circa 1900. The little wagon on the left is the first mail delivery wagon in Windham, with Clarence J. Vining the first mail carrier. The large beautiful house on the right was that of Col. George Robertson. The house was built in 1835 by William Young. Col. Robertson purchased the house in 1855 and soon after remodeled it to its present grand scale ("The Wedding Cake House"). Col. Robertson was to Windham what Zadock Pratt was to Prattsville. In over fifty years of his adult working life, Robertson was engaged in numerous tanneries, sawmills, merchandising, lumbering and farming endeavors. He did all that while running a temperance hotel east of Windham Village. He was an extremely wealthy and generous man, bringing prosperity to all who worked with and for him. The well-being of Windham was uppermost in his mind in conducting all of his business affairs.

Looking across the Mad Brook Bridge at the I. & H.G. Brockett Grocery and Dry Goods Store. Photograph circa 1905. Edwin Brockett came to Windham in 1855 and bought the store and post office of G.M. Peck, as well as the house just east of the store. His sons Irving, Harry and Charles ran the family business at some point in their lives for a total of about 90 years, selling to Edward Stead in the mid-1940s. The store was originally built about 1835 by William Young, who had a shop over the store. A shoe shop was added in later years and run by George Kelsey, and then by Lucius Graham.

Inside I. & H.G. Brockett's Dry Goods Store. Photograph circa 1915. Harry Brockett is waiting on customers.

I. Brockett,

DEALER IN

GENERAL MERCHANDISE,

Boots and Shoes

Fancy and Staple Dry Goods,

All kinds of Crockery and Glassware, and Furnishings of every description, Notions and Fancy Articles, Groceries and Provisions, Flour, Teas, Coffee, Spices and Country Produce.

POST OFFICE BUILDING, MAIN STREET, WINDHAM, N. Y.

Donovan Brockett at Five Years Old. Photograph circa 1906. Son of Harry and Jane Brockett, Donovan later ran the dry goods business for many years with his father. Donovan and his wife are the parents of Mary Brockett Holcomb.

The Art Bazaar. Negative, circa 1905. For the ladies in town, we now arrive at the fine store and home of Mrs. Jacob H. Wood. You will find here fine millinery, books, stationery and other fancy goods. This house was built before 1884 by Gary Baldwin and first occupied by Dr. Priest. Later it became the tailor shop of Ira Calkins.

Mr. Jacob Wood was engaged in a large meat market with D.S. Jones in the rear of the house for many years. By 1888 Levi Stead opened his meat market in this location. Mrs. Wood also opened an "ice cream saloon" in rooms adjoining her millinery store in 1886. By the mid-1920s the shop and house became a new boardinghouse known as The Mohican House, with James Hayden as proprietor

May 1908.

Dr. C.D. Mulbury of Windham tried an auto, but after a time sold it, and went back to man's best friend, the horse. An auto is an expensive, dirty machine for a doctor.

Main Street, Looking West across the Mad Brook Bridge. Glass plate, circa 1905. The attractive walking bridges on either side of the main road provided a continuation of the slate sidewalks that were laid throughout the village. To the immediate left are Mott's drugstore and George H. Davis's Billiards & Pool Hall. Next, to the west, was George Townsend's Central Hotel and Livery. On the right side is Patterson Bros. Grocery & Dry Goods Store.

Photograph circa 1890. Looking across the Mad Brook Bridge, we find A.R. Mott's Drug Store, George H. Davis's Centre Hotel and the Townsend Bros.' Central House.

The Central House was moved to this site by Samuel Miller in 1863. He enlarged what had been a butcher shop (Samuel was a butcher by trade) into the present hotel, to be opened as a public house known as the Eastern Hotel. In 1865 he moved to his premises the building known as the Gothic Hall and refitted it for a Town Hall. The hotel, while very successful, was sold many times. At one time this hotel was owned by Brockett & Seriver, Henry Mallory, and then H.A. Martin, who in 1876 referred to Gothic Hall as Centennial Hall. George Townsend purchased the hotel in 1886 and ran it for many years until George H. Davis purchased it around 1908.

Between the drug store and the Eastern Hotel was George H. Davis's Centre Hotel, Pool and Billiard Hall. He also ran a livery behind his hotel. This is the former home of Jerry Miller and then John Grant.

The Mad Brook Pedestrian Footbridge and Anson R. Mott's Gem City Pharmacy. Photograph circa 1890. The Widow Day resided here for some time and kept a candy and toy store. By 1878 the drugstore business was begun by Mr. Taft and, shortly after him, by F.D. Clum. Mr. Mott purchased the building in 1880 and had it entirely rebuilt as a store and residence by Rev. Wm. V. O. Brainerd, a carpenter as well as a man of the cloth. It was open for business by mid-1880. Beautiful Windham had become known as the "Gem of the Catskills," hence the Gem City Pharmacy.

1882 Windham Drug Store. 1882.

DRUGS & MEDICINES,

Fancy and Toilet Articles,

ESSENTIAL OILS, COLOGNES, HANDKERCHIEF EXTRACTS, FINE SOAPS, COMBS, BRUSHES, ESSENCES, TINCTURES, BARKS, &c.,

FINE CONFECTIONERY,

Best Variety of Stationery, Paper, Envelopes, Pens, Inks, Shelf Paper, Blank Books, &c.

SUNDAY HOURS FOR PRESCRIPTIONS. } 8 to 10 o'clock A. M. / 1 to 2 o'clock P. M.

Windham, Jan. 11th, 1881.

A. R. MOTT, Druggist.

GEM CITY PHARMACY

A. R. MOTT,

Druggist and Pharmacist

Prescriptions carefully compounded.

Staple Drugs and Sundries,

PAINTS and OILS.

WINDHAM SOUVENIR BAZAAR

Fancy Articles and Gifts.

CHOICEST CONFECTIONERY.

Chocolates and Bonbons, from Huylers, Brummels and Wallace.

FINE STATIONERY

FLAGS AND DECORATIONS.

Soda and Mineral Waters.

Main Street, - - - - Windham, N. Y.

" Gem City of the Catskills."

Inside the Gem City Pharmacy. Photograph circa 1900. The pharmacy was amply stocked with medicines, confectionaries, books, stationery, etc. To attend to customers, we find Daisy Tompkins Howard, Katherine Cole and pharmacist Anson R. Mott. There was also a beautiful white marble soda fountain.

April 1874.

The ladies of Windham are busy circulating a petition remonstrating against the sale of intoxicating beverages in this Town during the coming year. Many citizens are signing the remonstration. The purchase of Mr. Hill of the Osborn Hotel prohibits its sale there and it is urged that now is the time to stop its sale in town.

Photograph circa 1908. By 1908 the many improvements Mr. Mott has made to his establishment have greatly improved its beauty and size. His wife now runs a small boardinghouse in the rear with rooms for rent for $10–$15 per week.

In the building to the right, George H. Davis has opened his pool & billiard parlor adjoining his Centre Hotel.

Frank E. Holdridge with His Pleasant Valley Meat Delivery Wagon in Front of the Centre Hotel. Photograph circa 1908. Mr. Holdridge was a farmer and butcher by trade. He was also an innkeeper and proprietor of The Maples, a hotel east of the corner of North Settlement Road and Route 23 in Pleasant Valley. The Maples was in early times part of the Bump House complex run by Frank and Lucy Bump. Today it is the site of Cave Mountain Motel owned by Art and Jean Hammel.

A Local Republican Victory Rally. Photograph circa 1910. Republicans celebrate with a parade on Main Street. We find George Osborn Jr. with his goat wagon, which he used to give guests' children a ride around the Osborn House grounds. The goats are Teddy Roosevelt & Tom Platte. In front, left to right, are William Hill and George Osborn Jr. In rear are Leslie Soper and Raymond Thompson.

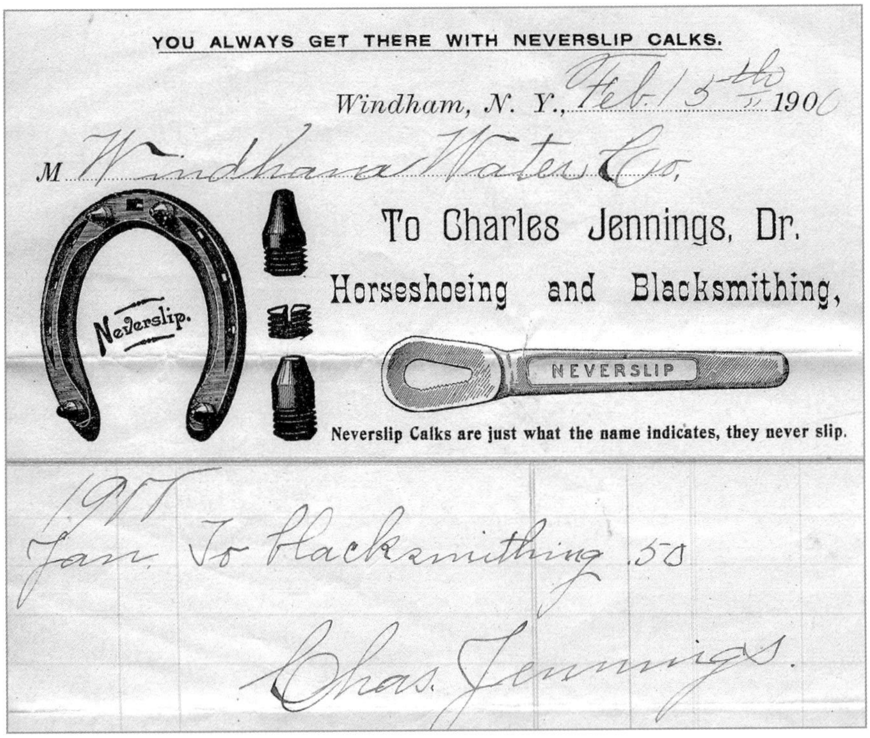

YOU ALWAYS GET THERE WITH NEVERSLIP CALKS.

Windham, N. Y., Feb 15th 1906

M Windham Water Co.

To Charles Jennings, Dr.

Horseshoeing and Blacksmithing,

Neverslip.

NEVERSLIP

Neverslip Calks are just what the name indicates, they never slip.

1905 Jan. To blacksmithing .50

Chas. Jennings.

Looking West along Main Street around 1900. Glass plate, circa 1900. Directly across from Mott's Drug Store we find an old landmark in Windham. In 1865 Gurdon H. Doty completed this fine building on what was then the corner of Nort Street (Mill Street) and Main Street. The lower floor was his blacksmith business, and the upper floor a paint room. Gurdon worked with his father, Captain William Doty, at blacksmithing and with his brother, Alfred, in the wheelwright business for many years. Alfred later gave up the wheelwright trade and studied dentistry. He and his son practiced dentistry in New York City, and in Windham in the summer. They built the little cottages on west Main Street between the present firehouse and liquor store. Charles Jennings took over as blacksmith from Doty in 1896 and was still in business in 1919.

April 1866.

Mr. George Baldwin of Windham has purchased the interest of E.W. Lewis in the celebrated and delectable summer beverage, "Cream of the Mountain" and is prepared to supply all who thirst after "pop."

Cole's Liveries!

K. M COLE, Prop'r, - WINDHAM, N. Y.

First=Class Conveyances for Light and Heavy Work.

Careful attention. Terms reasonable.

Enquire at DAVIS HOTEL, or LOWER MAIN ST. STABLES.

Negative, circa 1895. This beautiful maple tree–lined vision of Main Street taken just west of Mad Brook is typical of Main Street throughout Windham Village. These trees were courtesy of Col. George Robertson, a very successful businessman in the tanning industry, a farmer and hotel owner. As a good Christian and benefactor of the town of Windham, he had set out 900 maple trees along Main Street and a few miles east of town in the mid-1800s. Most, if not all of those trees are gone today, victims of old age, pollution from cars and the Main Street revitalization project in 2004. We can see Townsend's Central Hotel on the left, the Hitchcock and Patterson store on the right, and O.R. Coe's Hotel center rear.

Harold B. Moore's Garage. Negative, circa 1915. Harold is standing in the doorway. This building, next to and west of the drugstore, replaced George H. Davis's Centre Hotel about 1911. There were several owners early on. Cole & Osborn in 1911 had a Ford dealership. By 1914 it became George Arnold and Eugene Bailey's Central Garage. They sold Overland, Maxwell, and Ford cars.

In early 1915 B.G. Dewell and H.B. Moore took possession, for a short time, followed by H.B. Moore alone. The business became known as The Windham Garage. Moore also had Cadillac and Franklin cars for sale. He was a first-class mechanic.

Negative, circa 1895. This is a close-up of a picture of Hitchcock & Patterson's store. Note the large beautiful maples, the horse block and slated sidewalks. The old man and children are particularly interesting. This is the present site of Todaro's Salumeria.

1890.

Young men who hang around church doors Sunday evenings waiting to go home with the girls are called "Devil's Pickets."

The Windham Cornet Band in Its Fine Four-Horse Bandwagon. Photograph circa 1905. With no electronic games, TV, CDs, etc., to divert their attention, music became a very important part of a child's education and life. For the most part, girls attended singing schools taught by William Doty at one time, and the boys learned to play an instrument. Many young boys later joined their local cornet band, which almost every village and hamlet had organized. The larger towns, like Windham, were more fortunate in having their own bandwagon, which was used in many social and scheduled events during the year.

E.E. Munson is the driver. Truman Johnson is the drum major. Others, left to right: (front row) Benjamin Talmadge, Will Brainerd, Wray France, Mate Rogers, Will Stanley, Osborn Cole, Lewis Brockett; (back row) Edward Graham, Will West, Ralph Woodvine, Milton Dunham, Keeler Cole, Elbert Brainerd, Lemmie Mott.

The bandwagon is in front of Patterson Bros. Store on the corner of Mill Street.

WINDHAM MARKET,
LEVI STEAD,
DEALER IN
CHOICE BEEF,
Mutton and Lamb,
Pork, Sausage, &c.
And all kinds of
FRESH, SALT and SMOKED MEATS.
HOTELS, BOARDING HOUSES AND FAMILIES SUPPLIED.
Orders Promptly Filled.
Market, Cross Street near Main,
WINDHAM, N. Y.

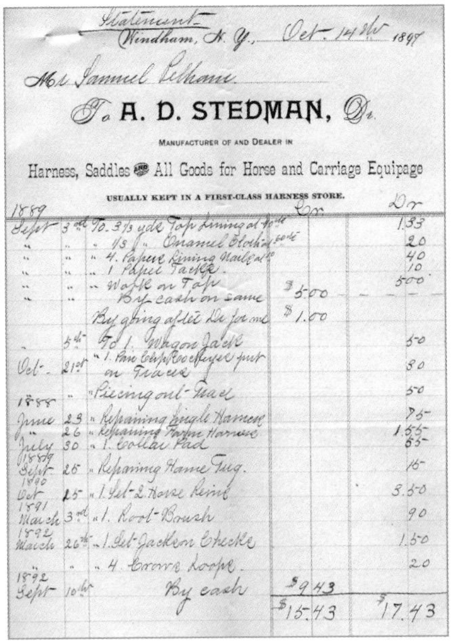
Statement
Windham, N. Y. Oct. 14th 1898
Mr Samuel Pelham
To A. D. STEDMAN, Dr.
MANUFACTURER OF AND DEALER IN
Harness, Saddles All Goods for Horse and Carriage Equipage
USUALLY KEPT IN A FIRST-CLASS HARNESS STORE.

RETURN TO
Daley & Talmadge,
Attorneys & Counselors At Law.
Over Hitchcock & Patterson's Store.
Windham, N. Y.
IF NOT DELIVERED IN 10 DAYS

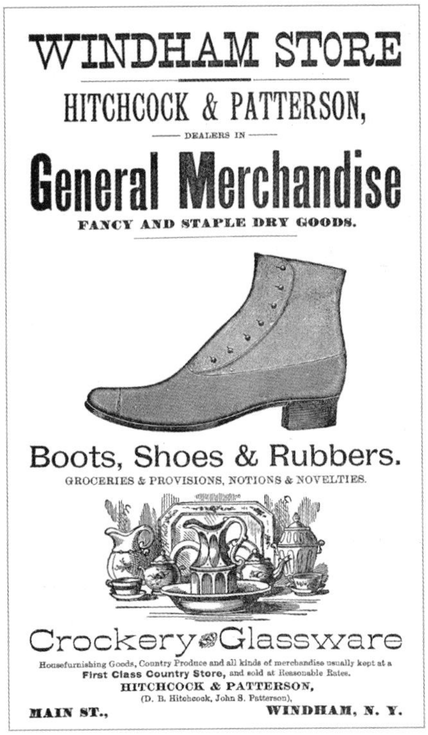
WINDHAM STORE
HITCHCOCK & PATTERSON,
DEALERS IN
General Merchandise
FANCY AND STAPLE DRY GOODS.
Boots, Shoes & Rubbers.
GROCERIES & PROVISIONS, NOTIONS & NOVELTIES.
Crockery & Glassware
Housefurnishing Goods, Country Produce and all kinds of merchandise usually kept at a
First Class Country Store, and sold at Reasonable Rates.
HITCHCOCK & PATTERSON,
(D. B. Hitchcock, John S. Patterson),
MAIN ST.,
WINDHAM, N. Y.

Hitchcock & Patterson General Store. Negative, circa 1895. Hitchcock & Patterson were in business together from 1881 until about 1895. At that time Patterson Bros. bought out Mr. Hitchcock. We do not know the occasion for the taking of this beautiful picture of the store and fine gentlemen.

This old building had upwards of eight previous owners since 1855, with many more to follow. There was a telegraph office here, and also the law offices of Daley & Talmadge on the second floor.

The building next and to the west of the general store is that of Mr. Charles Steadman's Harness Shop and upstairs residence that he built in 1851. According to the Windham Journal, *1881, "Go to Steadmans for the finest lot of whips, robes, blankets, trunks, valises and sleigh bells." In 1866 Steadman rebuilt the house next to and west of his shop into his residence. He sold that to Dr. P.J. Stanley in 1876. Today it is Bunce Realty.*

William and Edna Renz's Butcher Shop. Photograph circa 1929. This was located in the rear of the Munson & Ferris Corner Store on Mill Street and Main Street. Clarence Stead was a butcher by trade, just as his father Levi was, and worked for Mr. Renz for many years. Left to right: Clarence Stead, Edna Renz, William Renz, Nora Howard.

THE CATSKILL MOUNTAINS [Sixty-five]

WINDHAM, N. Y., IN THE CATSKILLS

The Paradise of the Catskills. High elevation, healthful climate, rugged scenery, macadamized roads, modern business establishments, excellent hotels and boarding houses, all amusements. On Mohican bus line.

THE CORNER STORE
All Kinds of Fancy Groceries and Fruits
MUNSON & FERRIS
Tel. 55F7
WINDHAM, - NEW YORK

AVERY'S DRUG STORE
THE REXALL STORE
ICE CREAM AND SODA
Served Right
H. T. AVERY, Ph. G.
WINDHAM, - NEW YORK

A City Store in the Mountains
We can fit you out in the most up-to-date clothing store in the Catskills.
MILLER BROS.
WINDHAM, - NEW YORK

The Windham Greenhouse Garden Cottage
Vegetable and Ornamental Plants
(A Christian Home)
Accommodates 10 guests
JOHN D. HOWARD
WINDHAM, - NEW YORK

BROCKETT & STRONG
Hardware, Sporting Goods, Auto Supplies
Gasoline, Oils, Greases, Auto Tires
Tel. 57-3
WINDHAM, - NEW YORK

S. G. McCOUBREY
General Electric Wiring System
Electrical Contractor
Jobbing and Contracting
Phone 60F4
WINDHAM, - NEW YORK

Cole's Pleasant View House
AND COTTAGES
On the Mohican Trail
Accommodations for 150 guests. Electric lights, telephone and all modern improvements. Lake and dance pavilion, affording all amusements, adjoining the premises.
Season May 29 to October 20.
Rates upon application.
MRS. TENNIE COLE
Telephone No. 56-F-6 Windham
WINDHAM, - NEW YORK

W. H. MOORE
Baggage and Express
Auto Livery
Phone Windham 55F13
WINDHAM, - NEW YORK

GOOD FURNITURE
at Reasonable Prices
FLOOR COVERINGS, PAINTS
OILS, VARNISHES
THE WINDHAM FURNITURE STORE
Cyrus R. Tibbals
WINDHAM, - NEW YORK

WINDHAM NEWS STAND
Souvenirs Stationery, Cigars and Candy, Soft Drinks and Ice Cream
Alle's Bus Station
P. C. VERMILYA
WINDHAM, - NEW YORK

DEYO'S MARKET
Prime Meats, Fish, Fruits Vegetables and Poultry
Phone 60 F 21
DANIEL DEYO
WINDHAM, - NEW YORK

GENERAL CASH STORE
C. DeLong, Mgr.
Full Line of Groceries, Fruits, Meat and Vegetables
Gasoline and Motor Oils
WINDHAM, - NEW YORK

THE THOMPSON HOUSE
I. THOMPSON & SON
A Modern House with the Home Atmosphere, Superior Cuisine, Spacious Lawns
Amusements for all
WINDHAM, - NEW YORK

WINDHAM GARAGE
HAROLD B. MOORE, Owner
Ford
THE UNIVERSAL CAR
Authorized FORD Sales and Service
Phone 55-F-2
WINDHAM, - NEW YORK

THE BLUE MOON GIFT SHOP
SOUVENIRS CONFECTIONERY
NEEDLEWORK
Clyde Adams Frances Adams
WINDHAM, - NEW YORK

HAYDEN HOUSE
THOMAS HAYDEN, Prop.
WINDHAM, - NEW YORK

JUNE 1869.

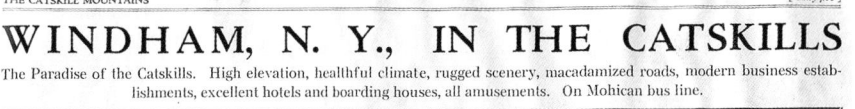

The 10th of July is the date fixed by the "Adventists" for the destruction of the World. Paper falling due on that date will therefore be payable on the 9th.

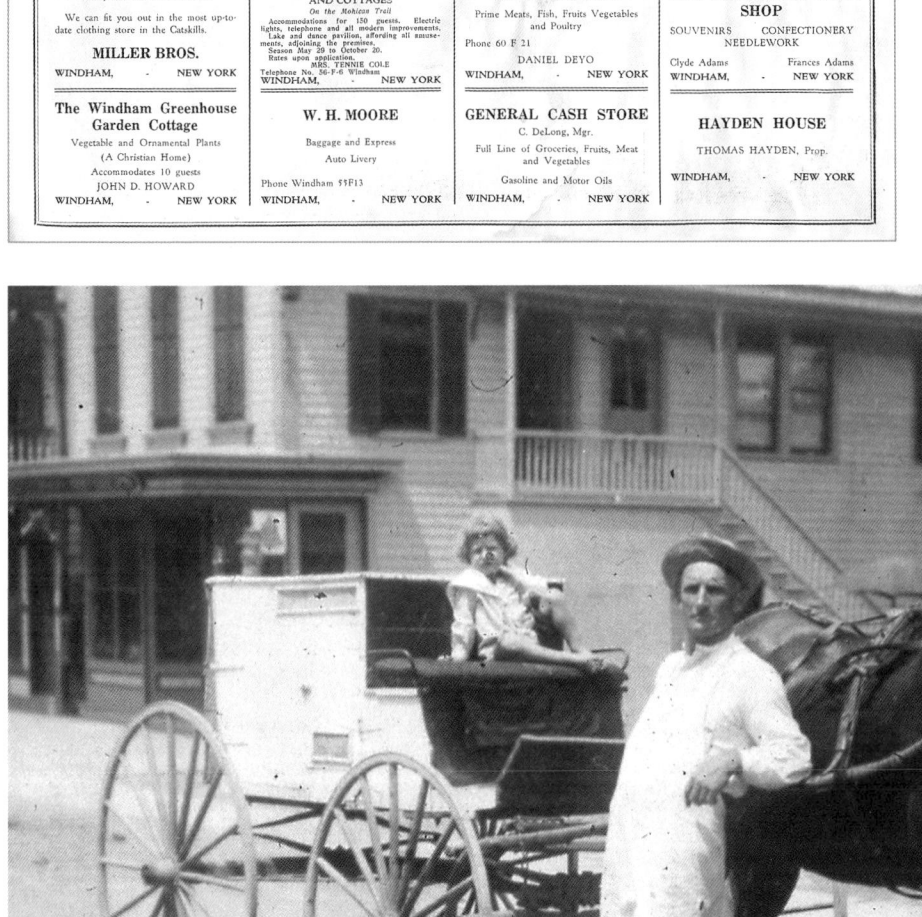

Clarence Stead and His Meat Delivery Wagon on Main Street. Photograph circa 1910. The little boy on the wagon is Clarence's son Edward. Edward went on to become a butcher like his father and then opened his own grocery store in the old Brockett store on Main Street.

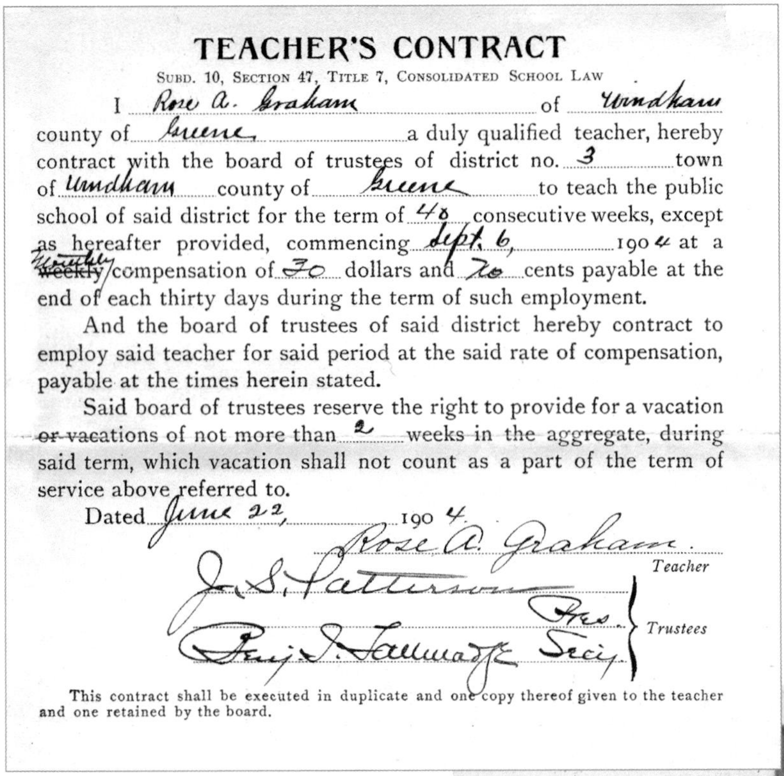

TEACHER'S CONTRACT

Subd. 10, Section 47, Title 7, Consolidated School Law

I Rose A. Graham of Windham county of Greene a duly qualified teacher, hereby contract with the board of trustees of district no. 3 town of Windham county of Greene to teach the public school of said district for the term of 40 consecutive weeks, except as hereafter provided, commencing Sept. 6, 1904 at a ~~weekly~~ monthly compensation of 30 dollars and 70 cents payable at the end of each thirty days during the term of such employment.

And the board of trustees of said district hereby contract to employ said teacher for said period at the said rate of compensation, payable at the times herein stated.

Said board of trustees reserve the right to provide for a vacation ~~or~~ vacations of not more than 2 weeks in the aggregate, during said term, which vacation shall not count as a part of the term of service above referred to.

Dated June 22, 1904.

Rose A. Graham. Teacher

J. S. Patterson Pres.
Benj. F. Tallmadge Secy. } Trustees

This contract shall be executed in duplicate and one copy thereof given to the teacher and one retained by the board.

June 1882.

A little boy who had been used to receiving his older brother's old toys and clothes recently remarked, "Ma, will I have to marry his widow when he dies?"

Village School District No. 3. Photograph circa 1895. The earliest school in the village was located near the old Brook Lynne Bridge on the Harmon Camp property. It was built of logs and heated with a fireplace. By around 1825 the school was located on Tibbal's Hill, corner of Mitchell Hollow and Main Street. In 1849 this new, two-story schoolhouse was built on the site of the present Masonic Hall.

From District School No. 3 to WAJ Central

In 1812 New York State recognized the need for formal education and established School Districts in the state to operate elementary schools for the first through eighth grades.

Most children attended school at least a few years, while some went on to complete eighth grade. Family obligations and work on the farm limited education for some. Most students remained on the farm or continued to live and work in the community and further education was not deemed necessary.

By 1880 there were 10 Common Schools with 300 students in Windham Township, corresponding to the township today. District School #3, one of these schools, was located on Main Street at the site of the present Masonic Temple. When compared to one room school houses, this was an impressive two-story building with more than one classroom.

By 1900, families recognized the need to further the education of their children. Through the efforts of Professor Lyons, District 3 became a Union Free School, with academic standing which allowed the teaching of high school subjects. At about the same time, a new school building was built on the same site which accommodated both elementary and high school grades. Children living in District 3 went to school here, attending grades nine and above free, the school tax paying for their education. Other districts in Windham, and other students from Ashland and Jewett townships, paid tuition.

In 1903, District 6 in Windham paid $100 for all its students to attend Windham Union School. Individual students paid between $5 and $10 tuition, many boarding in town while attending school. In order to attain accreditation as a Union School a library was needed in the school. In December 1900, the Windham Library Association transferred all its books, magazines and literature of every description along with bookshelves, tables and desks to the Union Free School for the sum of $1.

In 1903, the first six students graduated from Windham Union School. During these first three years, the Board of Education established graduation requirements as follows: 2 years (400 periods) English; 1 year (200 periods) History; 1–2 years (100 periods) Civil Government; 2 years (400 periods) Algebra and Geometry; 1 year (100 periods) Science and 6 weeks of Physiology.

The course of study was to extend to a minimum of three years, with at least 1,800 recitation periods of 30 minutes each. Teachers were hired for a 40-hour-week school year and were paid approximately $6.50 a week. In 1903, the school budget was $3,400.

In 1905, the New York State Dept. of Education informed Windham Union School that to advance the school to high school grade, the school must be in possession of a laboratory where individual pupils may perform science experiments. This was done by 1906 as was prescribed by law, and accreditation as a high school was given.

By 1913 the Dept. of Education decided that the school house was already too small and lacked proper equipment for its growing population. In July of 1913 the Board of Education presented a resolution to remodel its present school building for $5,000. This was defeated by the residents in attendance at the meeting by a vote of 43 yes and 45 no. During the ensuing months the Board of Education solicited bids for a new building on a different site. Catskill Supply Company gave an estimate of $13,500. The Board of Education decided that the most money it could raise through taxes was $9,500.

On Jan. 8, 1914, a resolution was presented to the public to erect a building for $13,500. This was defeated by a vote of 22 yes and 35 no. At this same meeting a vote was taken for renovations to the present school at a cost of $6,350. This was defeated by a vote of 16 yes and 40 no.

The state then advised the District that if it didn't erect a new school building, the school accreditation as a high school, and all supporting funds, would be withdrawn. On Jan. 29, 1914, the Board proposed a new building for $9,500 and this was passed by a vote of 71 yes to 46 no. The people also voted to sell the old building for $2,000 to the Masonic Temple.

During the summer and fall of 1914, the new school was built on the site of the current baseball diamond at WAJ Central School. To have the contract fall within the $9,500 appropriated, down from $13,500, the specifications were changed considerably, including eliminating the cupola and all ornamental work on the building. The new school came to be known as the "Cracker Box." It was opened in January of 1915.

By 1927 this building was again too small and additional elementary classrooms were built. Shortly after Centralization in 1931, a new school was deemed necessary and the present school was erected in 1936 for $275,000. It was to accommodate 400 students.

An addition was built in 1954 at a cost of $210,000 and in the 1970s the Butler Building was added. In 1986 a new gym, library and more classrooms were added at a cost of $1.2 million.

[*Windham Journal*, 1998. Article by Larry Tompkins compiled from school board minutes and records.]

1889.

Always wanted in this village [Windham] girls to do housework. About half of the girls here want to be school-marms and music teachers, and the remainder expect to marry rich men and be kept for dolls and have servants to take care of them. How sad their anticipations should they not be realized.

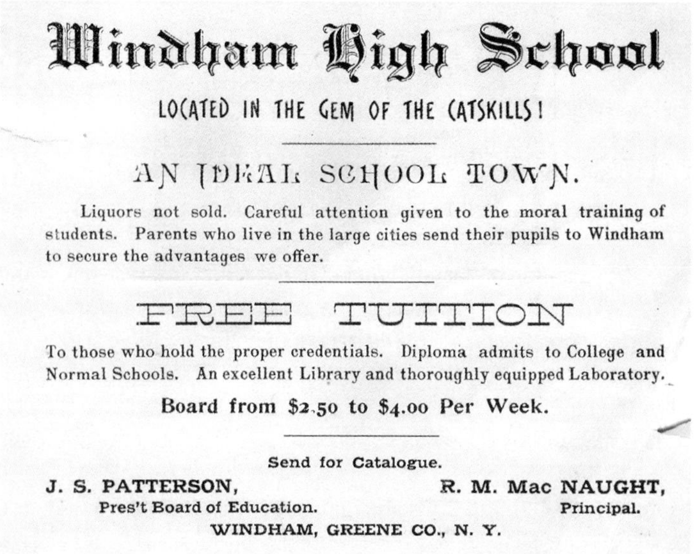

Windham High School

LOCATED IN THE GEM OF THE CATSKILLS!

AN IDEAL SCHOOL TOWN.

Liquors not sold. Careful attention given to the moral training of students. Parents who live in the large cities send their pupils to Windham to secure the advantages we offer.

FREE TUITION

To those who hold the proper credentials. Diploma admits to College and Normal Schools. An excellent Library and thoroughly equipped Laboratory.

Board from $2.50 to $4.00 Per Week.

Send for Catalogue.

J. S. PATTERSON, Pres't Board of Education.
R. M. Mac NAUGHT, Principal.

WINDHAM, GREENE CO., N. Y.

Windham Union School District No. 3. Postcard circa 1903. This school was built in 1900 to accommodate the growing village elementary student population and to further their education in high school subjects.

George Arnold's Home and Jewelry Shop. Photograph circa 1910. Mr. Arnold's shop was one of several jewelry stores in Windham over the years. In later years, around 1930, this was the home and business of Welcomb Moore, a dealer in feed and coal. Today it is Zerega's Pizza.

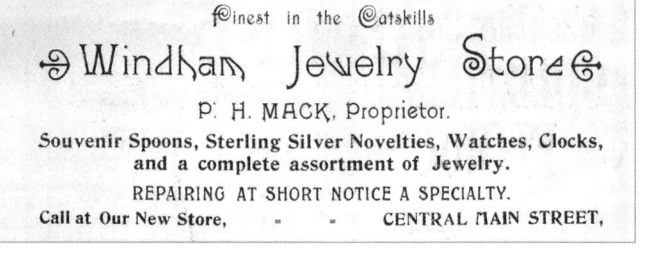

Finest in the Catskills

Windham Jewelry Store

P. H. MACK, Proprietor.

Souvenir Spoons, Sterling Silver Novelties, Watches, Clocks, and a complete assortment of Jewelry.

REPAIRING AT SHORT NOTICE A SPECIALTY.

Call at Our New Store, - - CENTRAL MAIN STREET,

Photograph circa 1910. This beautiful little building was constructed in 1899 by Pratt Brewer as a jewelry shop for Prentice Mack. In 1887 Prentice, known as the "Watch Tinker," had a shop in Hensonville, where in earlier years he was also known as the "Boss Horse Clipper." In 1901 he made an addition to his Main Street shop for John Jenne Jr. to repair bicycles. In 1927 the Windham Public Library purchased the jewelry shop, and the library resided here for over 60 years. Now it is the home of L.P.L. Financial Services.

September 1857.

Windham is a curious place. Its inhabitants have been so long ensconced within its precincts, that they are all in some way related! Let a stranger visit the place and speak ill of one of its citizens to another—ten to one that he is speaking to the third person's brother-in-law. Indeed, the ladies and young men all seek husbands and wives in the neighboring villages, because they don't believe in marrying their cousins.

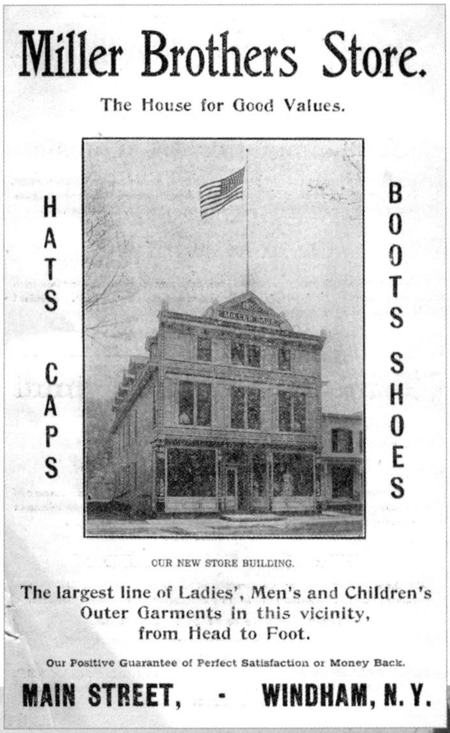

Miller Bros. Department Store / Windham First National Bank. Photograph circa 1925. When Harry Miller first came to Windham, about 1898, he opened his first dry goods and clothiers store in the Masonic Hall building farther west on Main Street. In 1906, with much success in the business, he bought the home of E. Graham and built a new department store incorporating the east end of the house into a large three-story building. Included was an Opera House for entertainment. The store had a soda fountain for many years, before it was moved to the Summit House in East Windham in 1919. In 1922 the First National Bank was built on the west side, incorporating more of the Graham house.

Home of Dr. Claude and Daisy Mulbury. Photograph circa 1909. This stately house was built around 1814 by Dr. Harvey Camp, the first doctor in Osbornville (Windham Village), who practiced from 1814–1860. The first doctor in Old Windham was Dr. Thomas Benham, who emigrated from Columbia County in 1793 to what is now the town of Ashland. Dr. Benham was very glad to have Dr. Camp on the mountaintop to help care for the ever-growing population of Old Windham, which he attended and traveled to on horseback.

Milo C. Osborn married a daughter of Dr. Camp and remodeled and made larger the old house circa 1870. Milo's son, Henry C. Osborn, carried on the milling business with his father for many years. Henry C. and Margaret Graham Osborn's daughter Daisy married Dr. Claude Mulbury, the second doctor to live in this house. In 1906 their son Edwin became the third doctor in the family and is still fondly remembered by residents today as their family doctor from years ago.

May 1876.

The Windham Cemetery is crowded so the inmates can't breathe, and an extension is called for. A generous next door neighbor will sell a half acre for $150.

Edwin Mulbury, Three Years Old. Photograph circa 1909. Edwin was the son of Dr. Claude Mulbury and his wife Daisy Osborn Mulbury.

Bennett's Bazaar, Dry Goods and Gift Shoppe. Photograph circa 1910. Bennett's store opened in 1907. In 1856 Levi Andrus had opened a shoe-making shop here. By 1880 Andrus had added dry goods and groceries for sale. In later years Harry Tiesmeyers ran a fruit, vegetable and fish market. In 1953 Janette McCoubrey had a gift shop and electric business here, followed by Doug Goff's barber shop, which operated for many years. Today it is the office for Dennis Hitchcock Builder.

Woodvine Cottage. Photograph circa 1895. This house, the home of Abijah Stone, was the third house built in Windham Village. In 1862 Moses White rebuilt the house into a boardinghouse, the first one in the hamlet. He called it Woodvine Cottage. It is now the site of a gas station on the corner of Church Street and Main Street.

Windham Centre Presbyterian Church. Negative, circa 1910. The Centre Church can trace its beginnings back to the First Congregational Church established in 1799 in Pleasant Valley. Known as the Old Meeting House, it serviced many denominations. As the settlements around Pleasant Valley grew, a need for churches in each settlement became necessary.

The Centre Presbyterian Church was erected in 1834 on land given by the Osborn family. This church served as a focal point in the community for many generations until about 1970 when it merged with the Windham Methodist Church to become the Windham Community Church, using the Methodist Church building for services.

In later years a group of concerned citizens formed a committee to preserve this beautiful building. The Centre Church is on the National Register of Historic Places and today serves the community as the Windham Public Library, Civic Center, and the Concert Hall, featuring the Windham Chamber Music Festival, one of the highlights of the summer season.

The Masonic Hall Building. Photograph circa 1903. This building has for many years belonged to Mountain Lodge 529 F and AM, which occupied the upper floor. The lodge was instituted on June 8, 1863, with Milo C. Osborn the first Master and with 157 members. In the mid-1820s, Bennett and Henry Osborn ran a store here. The first village post office was located here in 1831 with Bennett Osborn as the first postmaster. Windham was known as Osbornville at that time. By 1837 the name of the village was changed to Windham Centre.

In 1845 Matthews and Hunt opened a very successful carpet bag factory that lasted for many years. In later years the law offices of Raymond & Talmadge, and the office of dentist F.F. Frayer were here. In 1898 a very young Harry Miller came to Windham and opened up Miller Bros. Department Store here. He was so successful that he built his own store in 1906 on east Main Street.

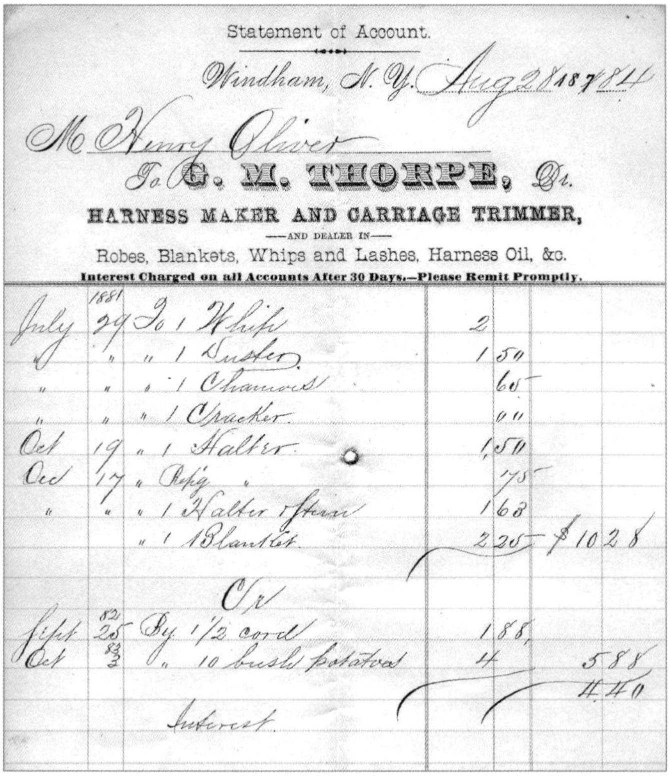
Statement of Account.

Windham, N. Y. Aug 28 1884

M Henry Oliver

To G. M. THORPE, Dr.

HARNESS MAKER AND CARRIAGE TRIMMER,

—AND DEALER IN—

Robes, Blankets, Whips and Lashes, Harness Oil, &c.

Interest Charged on all Accounts After 30 Days.—Please Remit Promptly.

1881 July	29	To 1 Whip	2	
"	"	" 1 Duster	1 50	
"	"	" 1 Chamois	65	
"	"	" 1 Cracker	04	
Oct	19	" 1 Halter	1 50	
Dec	17	" Repg	75	
"	"	" 1 Halter & stem	1 63	
		" 1 Blanket	2 25	$10 28
		Cr		
Sept 82	25	By 1/2 cord	1 88	
Oct 83	3	" 10 bush potatoes	4	5 88
				4 40
		Interest		

May 1870.

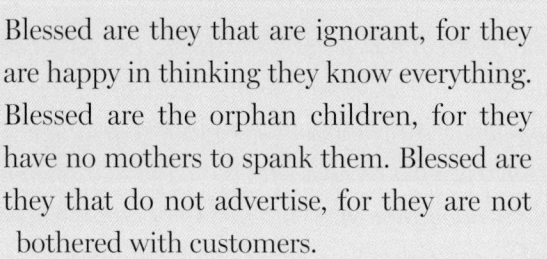

Blessed are they that are ignorant, for they are happy in thinking they know everything. Blessed are the orphan children, for they have no mothers to spank them. Blessed are they that do not advertise, for they are not bothered with customers.

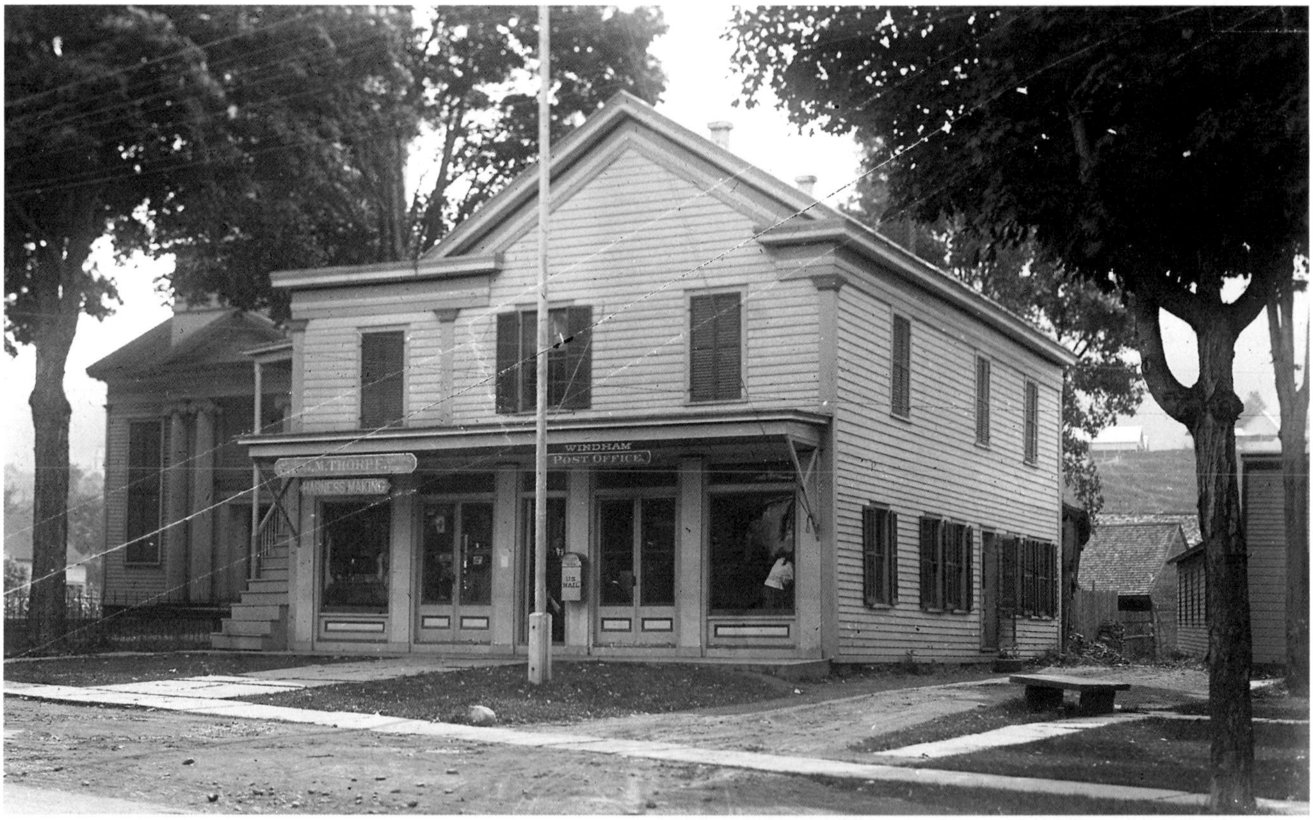

Granville M. Thorpe Harness Shop. Photograph circa 1910. Granville opened his shop here in 1876, in the east end of the building. The west end was occupied by the Windham Post Office at that time. In 1885 Albin E. West was postmaster and operated the post office in his clothing shop here. Postmaster was a political appointment that changed frequently, depending on the political party currently in office.

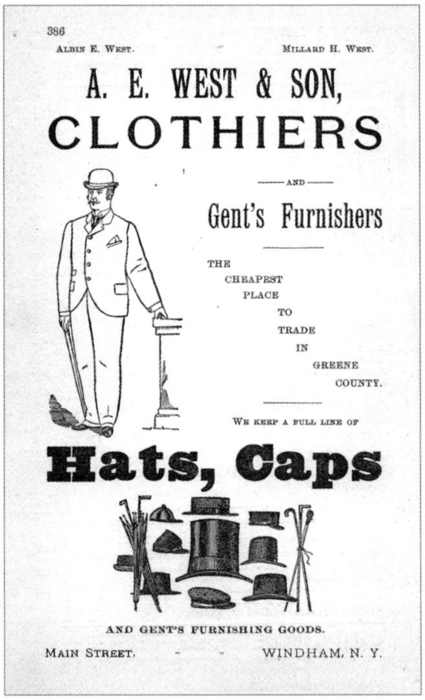

MARCH 1912.

The big bell in the Presbyterian Church Windham loosened from its moorings while being rung for Junior Endeavor meeting last Sabbath afternoon and dropped with a thud in the belfry. Fortunately no damage was done save the breaking of the frame which held the bell. It will, however, beckon saint and sinner to come to service next Sabbath.

Vermilyea's Souvenir Store. Photograph circa 1922. Pearl Vermilyea and Nina Moore ran a successful business here for many years serving the tourists who visited Windham. This is the same building as the G.M. Thorpe Harness Shop.

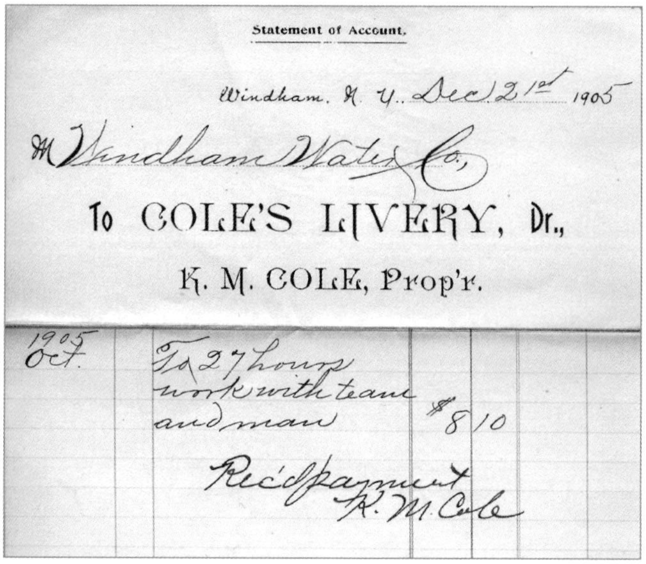

Statement of Account.

Windham, N. Y. Dec 21st 1905

M Windham Water Co.

To COLE'S LIVERY, Dr.,

K. M. COLE, Prop'r.

1905 Oct.	To 27 hours work with team and man	$8 10
	Rec'd payment K. M. Cole	

Coe's Hotel on the Mohican Trail

OPEN ALL THE YEAR

One of the Oldest Resorts in the

CATSKILL MOUNTAINS

Telephone 60-F-3. Windham, N. Y.
HENRY N. GIFFORD, Mgr.

Coe's Hotel, also known as Coe's Mountain Home, is centrally located in Windham village, in the heart of the Catskill Mountains, on the famous Mohican Trail, and is open all the year.

The house has all modern improvements, single and double rooms, with and without private baths; public baths, electric lights, running spring water on every floor, clean heated rooms, and comfortable beds.

The table is supplied with an abundance of fresh milk, eggs, poultry, vegetables, and other appetizing and home cooked food.

We serve the best that it is possible to produce, and make our charges according to the Golden Rule plan.

If we please you, tell your friends; if not, tell the Management.

O.R. Coe's Windham Hotel. Negative, circa 1881. First built as a house and store by Bennett Osborn around 1829, it was later converted to a hotel, the Osbornville House, and had no fewer than a dozen owners. O.R. Coe purchased it from George Ransom in 1878 for $2,600. Coe opened the hotel with 16 rooms in 1879 as O.R. Coe's Windham Hotel. By 1883 the hotel was four stories tall with sixty first-class rooms with numerous amenities. As with many hotels in its time, it was opened as a "temperance hotel." Somewhere along the line Coe changed the name of his hotel to Coe's Mountain Home. In January of 1906, Coe retired from the hotel business and traded his hotel for five unimproved lots in Palisade Park, New Jersey. This is now the site of Key Bank.

JULY 1860.

A. Newbury & Co. is now manufacturing the machinery necessary for chair making for Mr. Douglas of Hunter.

Windham Journal *Office. Glass plate, circa 1886. This was originally built by Noel P. Cowles around the 1840s as a mercantile business and was home to many other businesses over the years. The* Windham Journal *published its first issue in March 1857. W.R. Steele was the first editor. Editors changed frequently in the early years, as also did the place of publication around Windham Village. Today, in 2014, the newspaper is the longest operating newspaper published continuously under the same name in the State of New York. Many other businesses followed, including a Victory grocery store, a dry cleaners, and today, the Bistro Brie & Bordeaux restaurant.*

In this photo, Edward Cole, editor of the Windham Journal, *is sitting on the porch.*

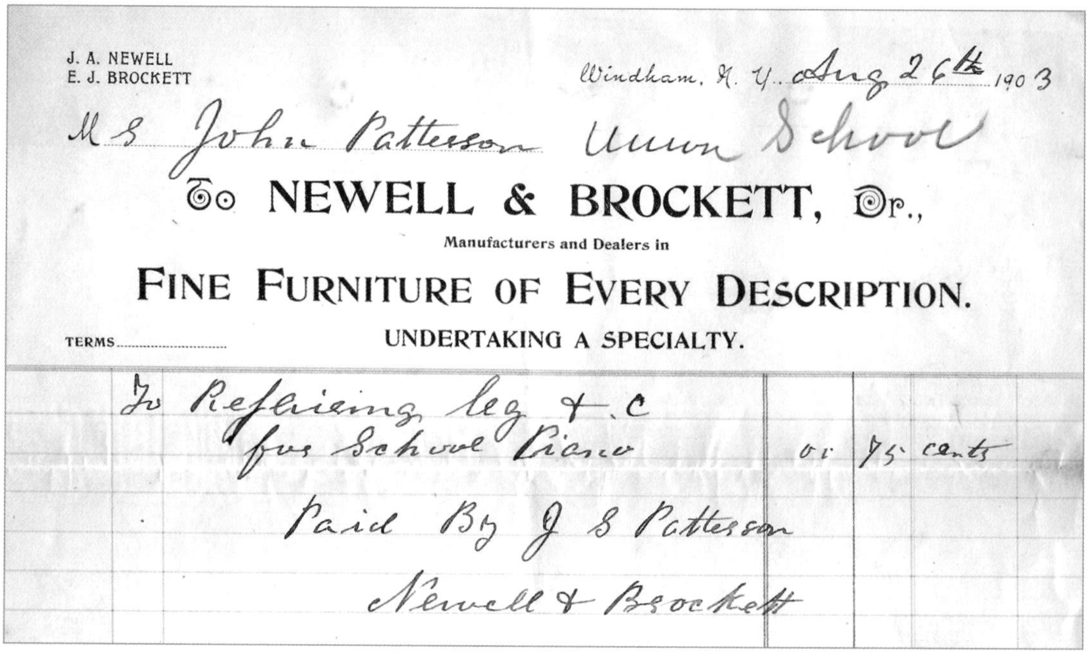

J. A. NEWELL
E. J. BROCKETT

Windham, N. Y. Aug 26th 1903

M S John Patterson Union School

To NEWELL & BROCKETT, Dr.,

Manufacturers and Dealers in

FINE FURNITURE OF EVERY DESCRIPTION.

TERMS..........

UNDERTAKING A SPECIALTY.

To Refairing leg &c for School Piano 0 75 cents

Paid By J S Patterson

Newell & Brockett

Ernest Brockett's Undertaking and Furniture Store. Glass plate, circa 1901. "Important Read!: Mr. Ernest Brockett of the firm of Newell and Brockett has successfully passed the exam to qualify him as a Licensed Embalmer. He is thoroughly qualified to do the arterial and cavity embalming, also the celebrated Dodge Needle Process. Competent and careful attention will be promptly given in all cases of death and burial." Windham Journal, *June 1901. This is now the site of the Bistro Brie & Bordeaux restaurant.*

Looking West along Main Street in Front of O.R. Coe's Hotel. Negative, circa 1912. Again we see the lovely maple tree-lined road, courtesy of George Robertson.

The building on the extreme right is the hardware store of Charles Brockett and Frank Strong. The store was built by S. Henry Atwater in 1887. Atwater was in the hardware business for a long time at the west end of town. He retired in 1890 when he sold the business to Brockett & Strong.

The building just west of the hardware store is the new firehouse, erected in 1911 on a 30'-by-100' lot purchased from Mr. Bump in 1909.

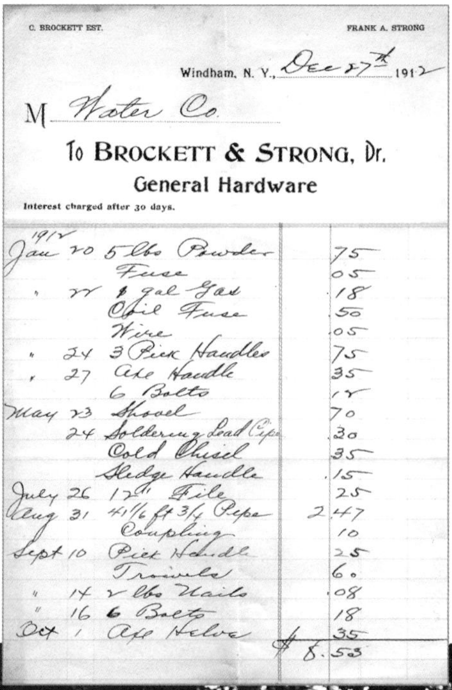

C. BROCKETT EST. FRANK A. STRONG

Windham, N. Y., Dec 27th 1912

M Water Co

To Brockett & Strong, Dr.
General Hardware

Interest charged after 30 days.

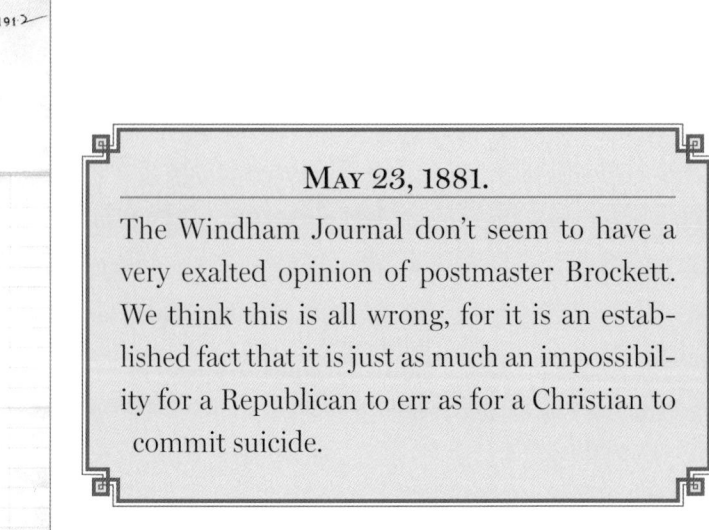

1912 Jan 20	5 lbs Powder	75
	Fuse	05
" 22	1 gal Gas	18
	Oil Fuse	50
	Wire	05
" 24	3 Pick Handles	75
" 27	Axe Handle	35
	6 Bolts	12
May 23	Shovel	70
24	Soldering Lead Cap	30
	Cold Chisel	35
	Sledge Handle	15
July 26	12" File	25
Aug 31	41/6 ft 3/4 Pipe	2 47
	Coupling	10
Sept 10	Pick Handle	25
	Trowels	6
" 14	2 lbs Nails	08
" 16	6 Bolts	18
Oct 1	Axe Helve	35
		$8.53

May 23, 1881.

The Windham Journal don't seem to have a very exalted opinion of postmaster Brockett. We think this is all wrong, for it is an established fact that it is just as much an impossibility for a Republican to err as for a Christian to commit suicide.

Looking East along Main Street near O.R. Coe's Hotel. Glass plate, circa 1918. The building on the right is the former home of the Windham Journal. *The hardware store is in the center. The firehouse, which served for over eighty years, is on the left. In 1916 the Windham Hose Company began showing moving picture shows, much to the delight of Windham residents. Walter J. Soper loaned his motion picture projector to the firemen for many years. Notice the iron fire ring to sound the alarm.*

Truman Johnson Home. Photograph circa 1900. Around 1800 a log house occupied this site, followed by a house/hotel built by Jessie Hollister around 1805, the first hotel in what was later to become Windham Village. Colonel George Robertson was born in this house in 1805. The hotel was also kept as a store for many years. The innkeeper manufactured potash a little to the east of this house on the future site of Noah Hill's livery stable, which today is located behind Windham Fine Arts Gallery.

This hotel was a welcome respite along the narrow, bumpy and dusty "almost roads" of that time. In later years this was one of several hotels and drovers taverns along the new turnpike. These establishments provided a bed that one might have to share with two strangers, but they also provided whiskey. Stills were everywhere on the mountaintop. This is probably what prompted the Temperance Movement in the mid-1800s through the early 1900s and the before-mentioned temperance hotels. Bennett Osborn kept this hotel for a number of years until he built the second hotel in the village, in 1829.

Lewis Mansfield, a furniture maker, then owned the house for some time until Truman Johnson purchased the building in 1871. Truman was a jeweler by trade. His family resided in Windham until 1944. Later occupants were Tom and Sue Stead and, later on, John and Carol Spear.

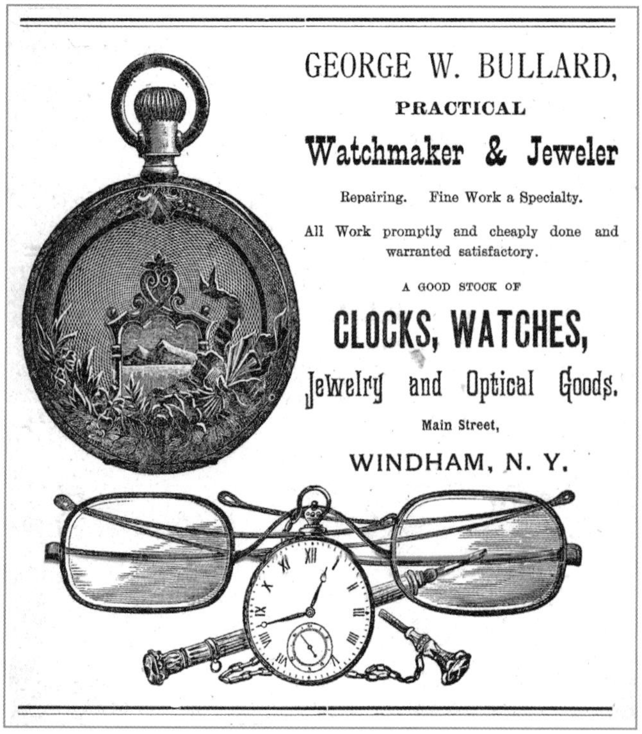

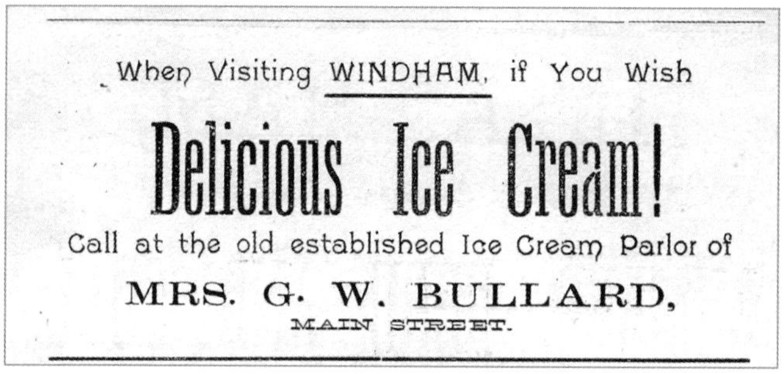

Jefferson Mead's Sap House. Photograph circa 1900. Next to and west of Truman Johnson's home is the Elm Cottage boardinghouse of Jefferson Mead, the inventor and patentee of the celebrated "Common Sense Carpet Stretcher." It seems it was a true wonder of the age. His house provided rooms for twenty guests. A farm connected with the house provided eggs, butter, fruit and chickens. There was also a "shaded glen park" with swings, lawn tennis and other amusements. That all these amenities were provided on such a small piece of property on Main Street is truly another wonder. Elm Cottage was also the former home of William McFarland, principal of Windham-Ashland-Jewett Central School in the 1960s.

Main Street Looking West near Windham Mills. Glass plate, circa 1895. Buildings left to right are: large building with columns is Potter & Newell's Furniture Store; third building over is Lawyer Mellen's Shoe Shop; fourth building is George Bullard's Jewelry Shop; last, M.C. Osborn & Sons Catskill Mountain Mills. These buildings were across from today's Windham-Ashland-Jewett Central School.

Bullard's building has a long and varied history. It was built for a mercantile business in 1831 by Daniel Hunt, who had many business partners over the years. Other owners were Kissock & Coons Marble Works, and there was also a tin shop here for many years. Later it became S. Henry Atwater's Hardware Store, in 1886, and then Bullard's Jewelry Shop. In 1892 Bullard shared his building with Jefferson Mead, who opened an Oyster Saloon. Mrs. Bullard had an ice cream parlor here in 1904. In 1930 Sam McCoubrey opened an electric appliance business here.

The Mill. Photograph circa 1895. This is another very historic building. It was built in 1810 by Bennett Osborn as a gristmill. By the mid-1830s the building was converted to a paper mill manufacturing straw wrapping paper, tea paper, printing paper and wallpaper. The mill was run by Macomber, Hunt and Olney until 1860, when it was purchased by A.B. Newbury Printing Press and converted into a foundry. The celebrated Newbury Printing Press was manufactured here and was used extensively throughout the country. M.C. Osborn and Eugene Raymond purchased the building in 1866 and reconverted it back into a very successful gristmill.

Left to right: (standing) ? Parkhurst, Graham Osborn, Margaret Osborn, Eugene Raymond, Louise Gannon, E.G. Graham (owner of the bicycle shop), Rev. C. Thorne, Ben Talmadge, Harvey C. Osborn; (seated) Glen Raymond, Irene Raymond, Alex Gannon.

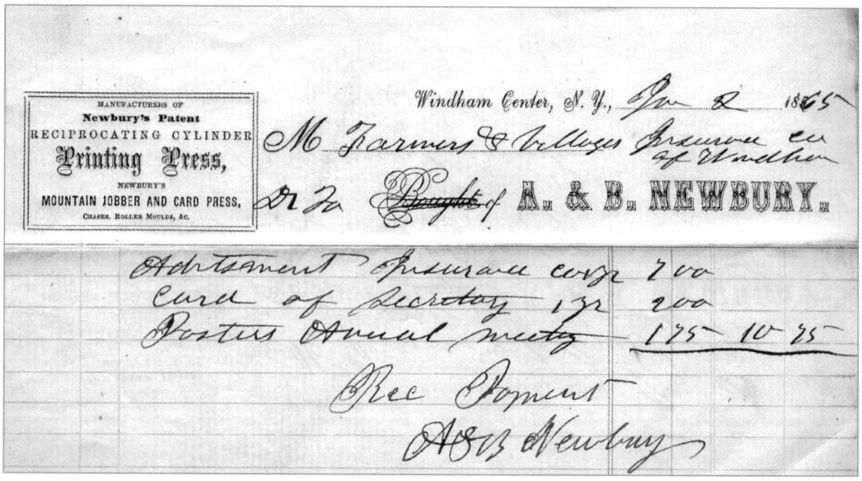

MANUFACTURERS OF
Newbury's Patent
RECIPROCATING CYLINDER
Printing Press,
NEWBURY'S
MOUNTAIN JOBBER AND CARD PRESS,
CHASES, ROLLER MOULDS, &C.

Windham Center, N. Y., 1865

M Farmers & Villagers Insurance Co of Windham

Dr To ~~Bought~~ of A. & B. NEWBURY.

Adrtisement Insurance comp	7 00	
Card of Secretary 1 yr	2 00	
Posters Annual meeting	1 75	10 75

Rec Payment

A&B Newbury

E.D. Blakesly's Variety Store. Photograph circa 1918. The earliest accounts have Lawyer Mellen operating a shoemaker shop here in 1856. E.D. Blakesly's Variety Store was here from 1916–1920. This was followed by three generations of the Morse family; Lorin, Grant and Richard Morse operated a very friendly, accommodating and successful grocery store until it tragically burned in 1976. Despite their loss, their love of Windham has kept the Morse family forever active in community and civic functions, helping to keep our sense of community alive.

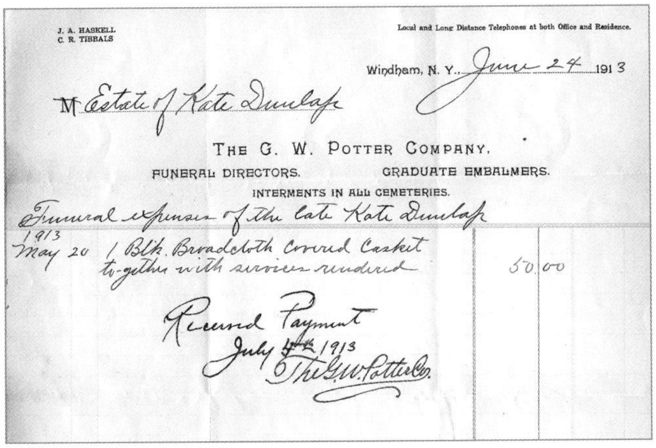
J. A. HASKELL
C. R. TIBBALS

Local and Long Distance Telephones at both Office and Residence.

Windham, N. Y., June 24 1913

M Estate of Kate Dunlap

THE G. W. POTTER COMPANY.
FUNERAL DIRECTORS. GRADUATE EMBALMERS.
INTERMENTS IN ALL CEMETERIES.

Funeral expenses of the late Kate Dunlap

1913 May 20	1 Blk. Broadcloth covered Casket together with services rendered	50.00

Received Payment
July 4th 1913
The G.W. Potter Co.

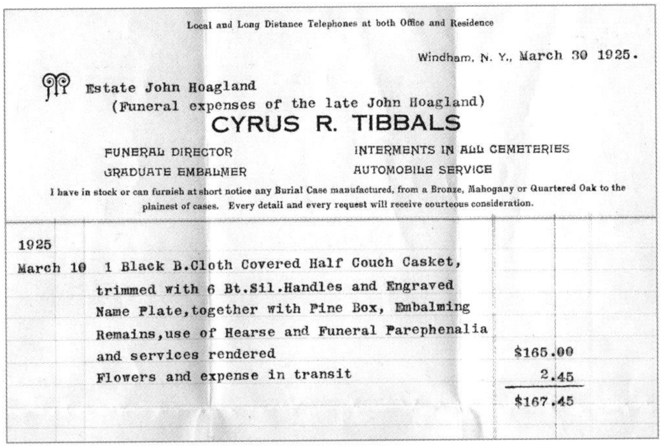
Local and Long Distance Telephones at both Office and Residence

Windham, N. Y., March 30 1925.

Estate John Hoagland
(Funeral expenses of the late John Hoagland)

CYRUS R. TIBBALS
FUNERAL DIRECTOR — INTERMENTS IN ALL CEMETERIES
GRADUATE EMBALMER — AUTOMOBILE SERVICE

I have in stock or can furnish at short notice any Burial Case manufactured, from a Bronze, Mahogany or Quartered Oak to the plainest of cases. Every detail and every request will receive courteous consideration.

1925		
March 10	1 Black B.Cloth Covered Half Couch Casket, trimmed with 6 Bt.Sil.Handles and Engraved Name Plate,together with Pine Box, Embalming Remains,use of Hearse and Funeral Parephenalia and services rendered	$165.00
	Flowers and expense in transit	2.45
		$167.45

Potter & Newell Furniture Store. Photograph circa 1900. All decked out for the 4th of July. George Potter served as an apprentice for his uncle, Humphrey Potter, in the mid-1840s. By 1856 George had bought out his uncle and continued his woodworking shop here. This lovely building was the largest furniture shop west of Catskill. John Newell went into partnership with Potter soon after, making very fine furniture and caskets. As their ad said, "Undertaking was a specialty."

In later years Cyrus Tibbals carried on as furniture maker and undertaker in Windham. By the 1960s George Winchell operated a laundromat here. It was lost in a fire in 1976.

Windham Union School. Negative, circa 1928. This was built in 1914 to teach high school grades and was dubbed The Cracker Box. An elementary school extension was built on in 1927.

The Briarwood House. Photograph circa 1925. In the earliest years, circa 1810, this was the home of Sanford Hunt and family, father of Washington Hunt. Washington was born in 1811 and became a lawyer and the Whig governor of New York State from 1851 to 1853. John A. Newell of Potter & Newell married Washington's daughter Eunice and resided here for a long time. In later years it was the home of the Minkler Family, then Robert Boughten. Currently it is the home of Graham and Kathy Merk.

*Negative, circa 1895. Continuing west along Main Street we are now in front of Potter and Newell's Furniture shop, on the extreme right. The next building on the right is the William Mansfield house, then the Wind*ham Journal *office. On the extreme left is the Minkler House. The stately house with columns is George Potter's house. This beautiful home was built some years earlier for Potter by Nowel P. Cowles, who built several homes and businesses in Windham. Cowles was a tailor by trade. As we have traveled through Windham, we have learned that most residents had more than one trade.*

George Potter learned furniture making from his Uncle Humphrey. An earlier venture had him opening an extensive dry goods grocery, hardware, clothing and medicine store near his house. That was too much work, so George bought out Humphrey's furniture store across the road. Potter's house is now the home of Bill and Nancy Ticho.

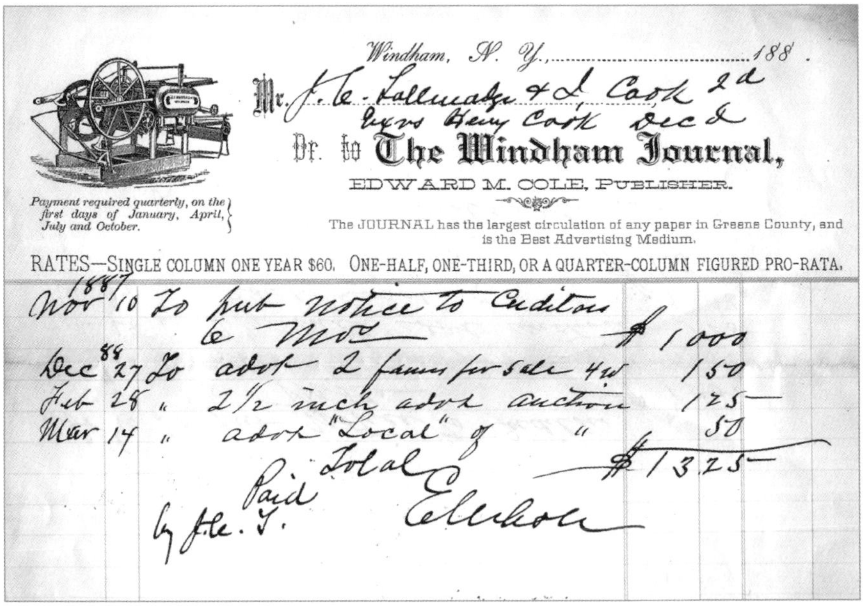
Windham, N. Y., 188 .
Mr. J. C. Tallmadge & L. Cook 2d
Exrs Henry Cook decd
Dr. to The Windham Journal,
EDWARD M. COLE, PUBLISHER.
Payment required quarterly, on the first days of January, April, July and October.
The JOURNAL has the largest circulation of any paper in Greene County, and is the Best Advertising Medium.
RATES—SINGLE COLUMN ONE YEAR $60. ONE-HALF, ONE-THIRD, OR A QUARTER-COLUMN FIGURED PRO-RATA.

1887
Nov 10 To pub notice to Creditors 6 Mos $10 00
88
Dec 27 To advt 2 farms for sale 4w 1 50
Feb 28 " 2½ inch advt auction 1 25
Mar 14 " advt "Local" of " 50
Total $13 25
Paid
by J. C. T. Ellicott

The Windham Journal *Office. Photograph circa 1921. This building was erected in 1873 by Edward Cole as a dwelling and, he thought, a permanent home for the* Windham Journal, *as he was the new publisher. The* Journal *was first published on the upper floor of Potter and Newell's before moving to six other locations in Windham. It occupied this building the longest, 70-plus years. In later years it was the home of Al Jergans' Phantazam, a photography studio. Keeler Cole, standing center, is Edward's son. The Cole family were owners of this building for 79 years.*

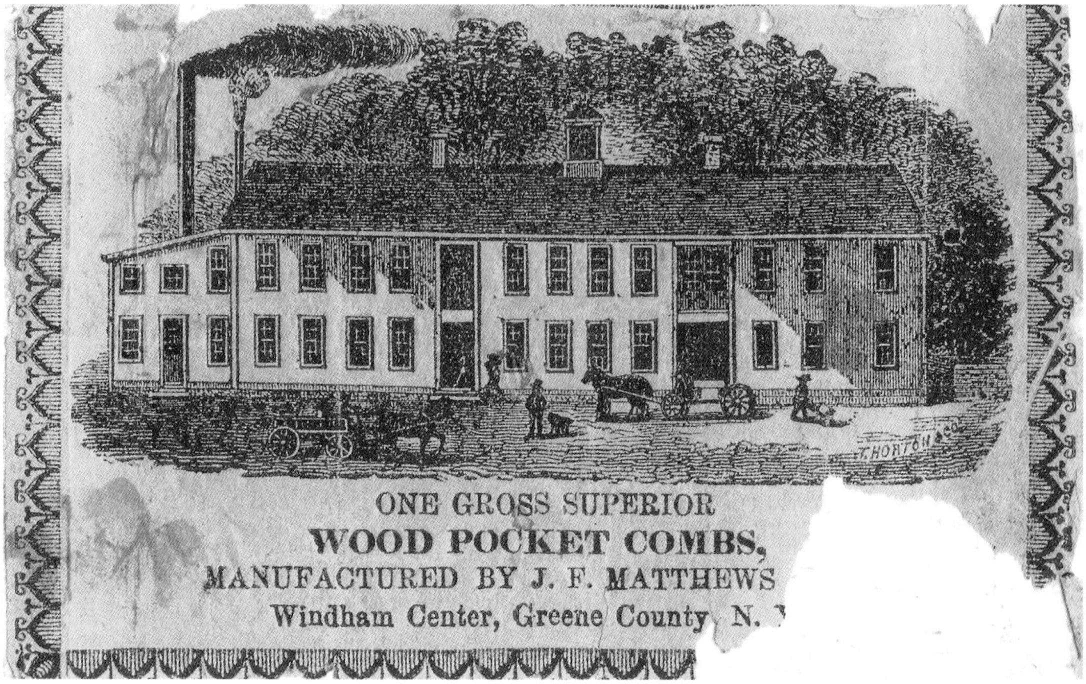

J.F. Matthews's Comb Factory. Barrel label, circa 1858. This large and impressive building was constructed by Jared Matthews circa 1845. He and his brother Edward began manufacturing buttons from wood and tin, later adding wood pocket combs, dressing combs and iron carpet bag frames. By the early 1860s Jared sold his interest to Edward. Jared moved to just west of the village and began to manufacture broom handles and brooms.

The old factory was taken over by Mr. Hart in 1867. He began a woolen factory, making flannels, cashmeres and satinets. In 1869 the building was sold at auction to S.P. Ives for $1,100. It remained empty until 1873, when Ahaz Cole and his son Edward purchased the building. Edward began taking down the building piece by piece. He used the material to build a fine home for himself (now the law office of Sean Doolan) and another building just east of his house to be a residence and possible future home of the Windham Journal, *of which he now owned half-interest. The* Windham Journal *occupied that building until 1995.*

The Alphonso Cobb House. Photograph circa 1910. This lovely home was built by N.P. Cowles circa 1856 for Mr. Cobb, a longtime resident. Cowles built many homes and businesses in Windham Village. More than sixty years ago Dr. Robert Blakeslee and his wife Josephine purchased the house and raised five children here.

John Howard's "Garden Cottage." Photograph circa 1910. This beautiful home on the west end of Main Street was built circa 1852. Around 1900 John Howard and his wife Mary Brandow purchased this small farm and called it Garden Cottage. John's love of horticulture led him to open a greenhouse and garden shop. Pictured are John, Josephine and Mary Howard.

Their daughter Josephine married Ernest Van Valin, and they continued the nursery business, as did their son Philip. Philip was one of the nicest gentlemen in town, always friendly and helpful. The Van Valin family was in business for more than 90 years. They sold the property to Drew and Natasha Shuster in 1995, who still sell flowers and vegetable plants, as well as many other items, at their Catskill Mountain Country Store. Eleanor Burrows-Hoare and family lived here for a short time in the late 1990s.

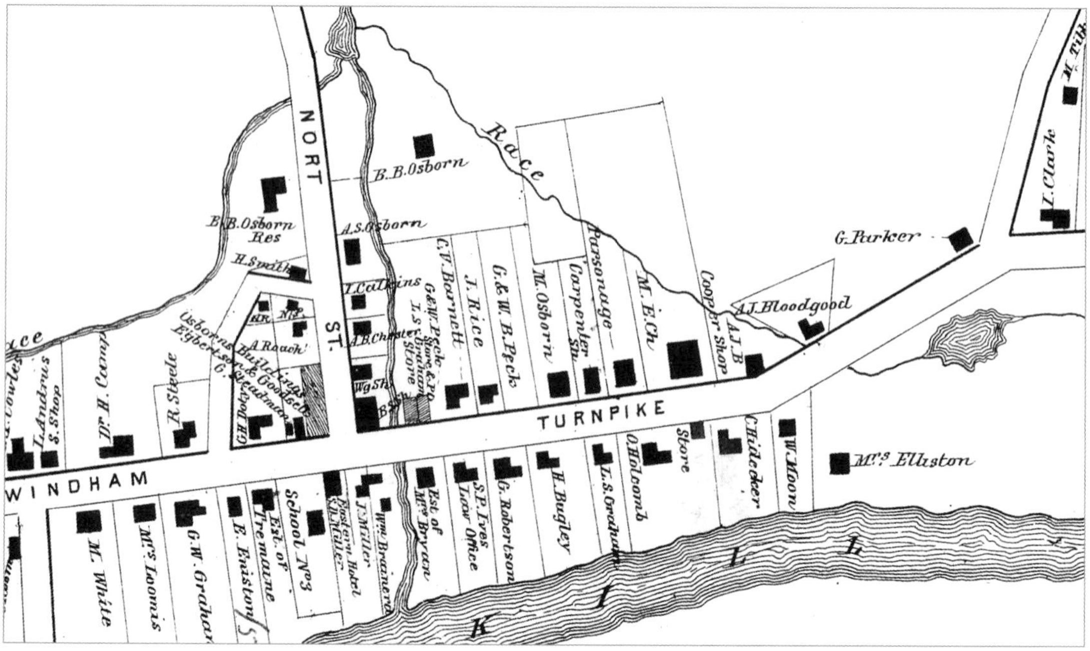

East end of Main Street, Windham, 1867.

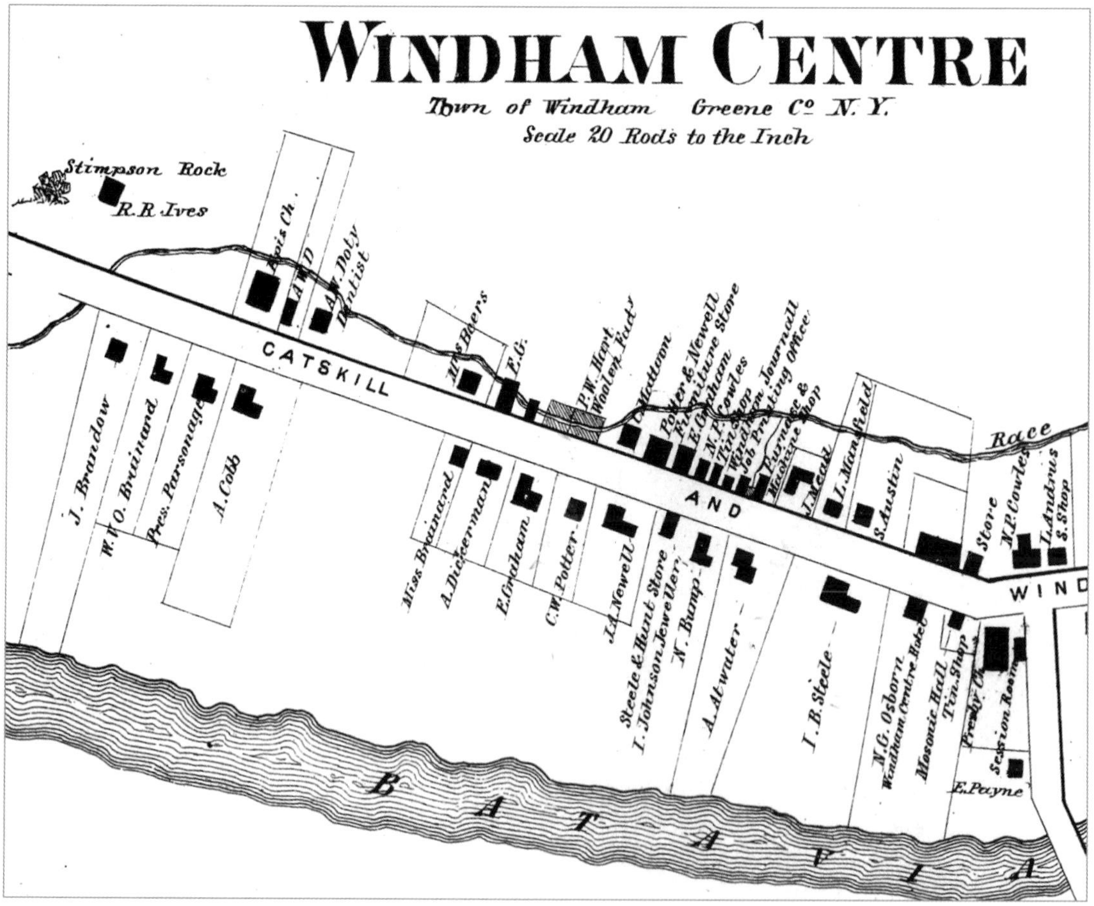

West end of Main Street, Windham, 1867.

Around Windham

Even before the mountaintop was divided up into the different townships we know today, the early pioneers gave names to many of the settlements where a number of families took up residence—Union Society, Mitchell Hollow, North Settlement, South Street Settlement, to name a few. Each of these settlements had its own history.

When these early settlers came to the mountaintop, they were all looking for a new life and a new beginning in new territory. They were not concerned with whether they were the first, second, or even the tenth settler in the area. They were just happy to be there. When the early history of the mountaintop was written in books or personal family histories, the use of the adjective "first" became a very prominent word applied to churches, businesses, schools and every other structure and endeavor. It is very difficult to easily document with accurate dates, however, many

Pelham Homestead. Photograph circa 1910. Another pioneer family settling in Windham in the early 1800s was the Pelhams. There were a number of Pelham family farms on the Old Road area of Union Society. The farm pictured here is that of Joseph Pelham, son of Isaac Pelham, who first settled in Windham.

Joseph is standing, extreme left. His son James LeRoy and James's wife Katherine Albright are seated. Their son, Walter J. Pelham, three years old, is in front. The other people are boarders at the house. Joseph is the great-great-great-grandfather of the "Pelham boys"—Michael, Bobby, Ricky, Thomas, and Dykeman—and their sister Judith.

Joseph's brothers, William, Steven, and Samuel, each had a farm on Old Road in 1897.

of the events before and around 1800. Suffice it to say that between 1785 and 1795 there was a great migration westward to the Catskills. In many cases the difficulty in passing through the dense forest and over the steep mountains precipitated the settlement in any valley with level ground that the pioneers happened upon. The photos in this chapter transport us to the northern regions of Windham Township as well as to the South Street Settlement near the village of Windham.

Old Road School District #10. Photograph circa 1897. This school was located on the northwest corner of the junction of Old Road and Galway Road. The teacher at this time was Terry Parker. Left to right: Hilda Albright, Harry Ostrander, Clayton Miller, LeRoy Miller, Sam Tompkins, Brayton Tompkins, unknown, unknown, Blanch Miller, Sheridan Cammer, Francis Tompkins, Earle Ostrander, George Albright.

Old Road School District #10. Glass plate, circa 1912. The teacher at this time was Miss Brainerd, but we do not know the names of the children except for one. The boy in the center, third from right, is Clarence E. Tompkins, my father. Some of the boys in the picture are Pelhams.

Wallace Cammer. Glass plate, circa 1900. Near the top of the hill on Old Road is the Wallace Cammer farm. We find Wallace with his simple, but very effective, stump puller—just part of the arduous task of land clearing on a small farm. This, along with the clearing of thousands of rocks, needed to done to create pastureland. The rocks that were removed were used to mark boundary lines along a neighbor's property.

Overlooking Windham from Cammer's Hill. Photograph circa 1925. This photograph looks west from the top of Cammer's Hill and the Wallace Cammer farm. The house in the foreground is the J.M. Barkley place, at the corner of Nauvoo Road and Old Road. The buildings at lower left are Cole's Pleasant View Resort on Route 23. The buildings at upper left are the Munson House Resort. Just to the right is Elmer Munson's Crest Park. The village of Windham is right-center.

J.M. Barkley House. Postcard circa 1910. From yet another pioneer family of Old Windham, we come to the Lemuel Stimpson house at the juncture of Old Road and Nauvoo Road. In this early time the upper end of Nauvoo Road was referred to as Stump Hollow. This reference is to the tanning industry on the mountaintop and the millions of trees cut down for their bark, leaving the kind of stumps that Mr. Cammer had to remove in order to create farmable land.

In the 1920s the property belonged to James and Edith Barkley. At one time Edith ran a concession known as the Orange Tea Room. By 1948 the property was bought up by Dr. Porcello. The house is still in his family and now owned by Claire Porcello Davis.

Stone Crusher. Glass plate, circa 1906. In this wonderful photograph, near the corner of Old Road and Route 23 we find a steam-driven stone crusher. By 1900 most main roads that were all dirt were being covered with crushed stone. They are resurfacing the old turnpike here. At this site, made up mainly of rock ledge ready to be crushed, a new and more permanent roadbed could be made. By the 1920s on-site rock crushers were not necessary because of the advent of paving,

By the mid-1920s John and Florence Antun built a summer cottage on this location and it is still in use today by Joan Antun Redner and her family.

Cole's Pleasant View House

WINDHAM, GREENE CO., N. Y.,
A. COLE & SON, Proprietors.

Accommodates 60 Guests.

No more pleasant resort in the Catskills. Large rooms with transoms. Gas light. Farm coneected with House. Long distance telephone in House. Ten minutes' walk to churehes, stores, telegraph office, physicians, etc.

Terms $8 to $10 Per Week.

A beautiful Glen is connected, where many city people ramble each season. A good Livery is kept for the accommodation of guests. Excellent roads and many interesting drives in the vicinity.

Send for our little descriptive Booklet.

Cole's Pleasant View House. Photograph circa 1920. The northwest corner of Old Road and Route 23 is the site of the old Elias Reynolds Place. Reynolds is an old family in Windham dating back to 1804. Elias had made his fortune in iron mines in Ancram, and in the mid-1800s ran this large farm. When he was older, he sold the farm to John M. Cole in 1888. Cole built the large boardinghouse pictured, which was run by members of the Cole family until the late 1950s. In 1923 Osborn Cole developed Cole's Glen Lake on Reynolds Creek behind the main house.

Millard Cole sold the property to the William Pelham family in 1958. The Pelhams ran the boardinghouse until the mid-1960s, when it was sold to the Lucas family. In more recent years the main house was torn down. In 1959 William Pelham built the long-popular Pleasant View Lounge and Restaurant.

August 1901.

The town has a host of strangers "within our gates." The influx is big and the hotel men are happy. This is as it should be for Windham is the "loveliest village of them all" and it is a remarkably healthy town, moral, intelligent industrious people. Our dales and hills present an ever changing panorama, and bring back to the sick the ruddy hues of health.

Frank Dunham and Team. Photograph circa 1890. Frank Dunham joins a long line of teamsters since 1800 to ply the roads from Windham to Catskill. Frank was very proud of this heavy wagon drawn by his grand horses three abreast. Teamsters were in great demand to draw country produce such as apples in barrels, tubs of butter, potatoes, grain from the mills, woodenware from the carpenter shops, etc. On his return trip his wagon would be piled high with every conceivable kind of merchandise in use at the time. Sometimes not finishing his deliveries until midnight, he arose at first light only to repeat the process again.

Frank and his wife Lucy are the parents of Carrie and Mary Dunham.

The West House. Photograph circa 1900. This house, located on Mitchell Hollow Road, second house on left, is the homestead of Nicholas Edward and Carrie Sutton West. Like his father, Albin E. West, Nicholas learned the trade of millwright, working at Osborn and Sons Mill on Main Street. Nicholas had the privilege of working under William Woodvine, considered the most experienced miller in the country, understanding every aspect of the operation of a flour mill.

In this picture we see two of the women of the house doing laundry in an old wooden tub. One daughter of Nicholas West was Anita Lucretia, who married Ferris Thompson and worked at the Thompson House most of her life.

Valley Brook Farm. Photograph circa 1914. We have arrived at the Valley Brook Farm, our first stop on Mitchell Hollow Road, with the Arthur and Sarah Austin family lined up to greet us. Left to right: Clarabelle, Alice, Sarah, Arthur, Stella on lap, Edna, Garwood, Ethel, Merrill. Garwood would become a master carpenter, building many homes and businesses on the mountaintop. It is very appropriate that Merrill is standing with a horse. After owning and running the old Branaugh Farm on the west end of Windham Village for many years, he took up raising trotting horses and racing them at Saratoga very successfully. Merrill is the father of Peggy Austin Sokoll of Windham.

The Hayden House / "Bell House." Photograph circa 1925. In 1808 Jonathan Bell, his wife and family emigrated from England to Windham. He built this beautiful stone house with four chimneys on Mitchell Hollow Road in 1827. He and his son Joseph farmed the homestead their whole lives.

In 1865 Julius Fairchild purchased the farm. By the time of the marriage of his daughter Ella M. Fairchild to John Hayden, the Hayden House had begun as a business. After a large addition was added, it became one of the finer boardinghouses in Windham. In later years it was the home of the Hans Deppe family and, even later, of Dieter Steinman.

Upper Mitchell Hollow Schoolhouse. Photograph circa 1922. At the corner of Mill Street and Mitchell Hollow Road stands this 1830 schoolhouse, referred to as "the red schoolhouse" in early days. This school is on the site of an earlier school that burned down in 1829. The schoolhouse had a pulpit about twelve feet in height, and the building was used for church services in early years.

The teacher is Mrs. Kitty Doolittle. The students are, left to right: (back row) Shelden Maben, Carl Vining, Walter Coventry, Lenard Cleveland, Milton Case, Myron Case, Harold Finch; (front row) Daisy Sebolt, Hazel Sebolt, Helen Cleveland, Louise Vining, Margorie Maben, Stephen Bernhard.

August 1875.

There are plenty of girls who are too feeble to drive a broom over a dusty carpet, but they can swing a croquet mallet with the force of a pile driver.

Mitchell Hollow Chapel. Photograph circa 1935. As it became more difficult to hold services in the schoolhouse across the road, the congregants decided in 1897 to build their own church. Everyone contributed with money and labor. By April 1898 the church was built and paid for. The official name was The Mitchell Hollow Society Chapel, welcoming all denominations. Some of the old families who worshipped here and made this chapel possible were the Tuttles, Doolittles, Mabens, Cases, Howards, and Lanes. The Vidbel family has long been active in protecting and preserving the church. Leola (Dutch) Lane and Joyce Vidbel have been especially devoted to its preservation.

AUGUST 1874.

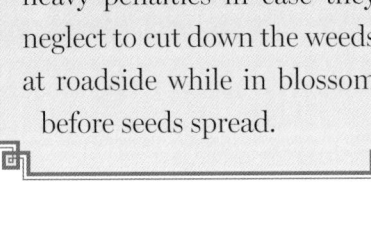

Path masters will do well to remember that by existing statute they are subject to heavy penalties in case they neglect to cut down the weeds at roadside while in blossom before seeds spread.

Burton Robinson and Meuta Ann Brockett Robinson. Photograph circa 1895.

Robinson House. Photograph circa 1895. This is the home of our hosts, Burton and Meuta Ann Brockett, in upper Mitchell Hollow. Formerly it was the C. Edgar Brockett farm. This house may very well be the one sometimes referred to as the Old Mitchell Place. The little boy is Robert Edgar, who died soon after this picture was taken.

Burton Robinson married a second time, to Juliet Young, in 1912. They are the parents of Cleo and Andrew Robinson. Cleo, an explosives expert in the building of the Holland Tunnel, is the father of Robert and Suzanne Robinson, who went to school in the Windham-Ashland-Jewett School District in the 1950s and 1960s.

Chester Alberti House. Photograph circa 1912. This is another old homestead, that of the Nelson family who settled in Mitchell Hollow in 1824. It was a large farm of 115 acres, which was passed on down in the Nelson family until 1909, when Merritt and Kate Alberti purchased the farm. Merritt's sons Chester and Robert later operated the farm for many years. Robert still lives on the old homestead. Notice the picket fence, built to protect the front yard and house from wandering cattle during drives to market.

Old Milk Wagon. Photograph circa 1915. Elmer Lobdell and his wife Elizabeth are on their way to the creamery in Windham Village. Considering how nicely she is dressed, Mrs. Lobdell must have other plans besides a milk run. Their farm was near the junction of Mitchell Hollow Road and County Route 10.

Mount Pisgah. Photograph circa 1910. This beautiful day finds the Cammer and Conine families on an outing at the top of Mount Pisgah. The log cabin behind them is that of Walter Doolittle and family, who moved from Rensselaerville in 1880. The family built a mile-long road to the summit of 2,900-foot Mount Pisgah and built a two-story cabin. The Cammers and Conines were here to see the magnificent views from the observatory.

Left to right: (front row) Shirley Cammer, Rosellia Cammer, Sheridan Cammer, Estell Cammer with baby Ceila Conine, unknown with unknown baby; the two children in front are Shirley and Harold Conine; (rear) Mrs. David Cammer, David Cammer, Wesley Cammer, unknown, unknown, unknown, unknown, unknown.

Mount Pisgah Observatory. Photograph circa 1890. In 1880 Walter Doolittle bought 275 acres on the top of Mount Pisgah, where he first built a log cabin. Within the first year he built a two-story house for his family, bringing the materials up the mile-long road that he had built as well. He then began taking in guests in late 1881.

The view from the cleared mountaintop was 360 degrees and spectacular. To enhance the view and the pleasure of the many visitors who made the trip up, Doolittle built a two-story addition to the house with a fine observatory on top. He also spent $100 on the latest telescope for star-gazing.

With the latest improvements made in the early 1920s, Pisgah Cottage could accommodate thirty guests. There was a separate building used as a dance hall and for other amusements. There was also a race track around the perimeter of the mountaintop. The hotel was consumed by fire in 1925. It was never rebuilt, and the forest reclaimed the site.

Mount Hayden House. Postcard circa 1905. This property in the late 1700s was the John and Clarke Twist farm. By 1860 Thomas Hayden had purchased the property and built this very large house to accommodate the many children he had with his wife Bridget Murray. In later years, as his children grew up, Thomas and son James transformed his home into a boardinghouse. The farm was at the very top of what is now Begley Road, on a mountain that was later named for the Hayden family. The house is long gone, and Windmont Development now occupies the site.

The Benoni Austin Farm. Photograph circa 1910. Located on the early Durham-Windham Turnpike (County Route 10), this house was built circa 1840 by Wells Finch, a farmer. It was owned by Daniel Ingraham in 1856. By the late 1800s Joel Austin owned the farm, followed by his son Benoni and his wife Clarabell, all hardworking, industrious farmers.

About 1937 William Kelly and his wife Lulu Wetmore took over the farm and opened a boardinghouse named Kelly Acres. Lulu's grandson, Steven Walker, and his wife, Nancy La Pietra, continue the homey boardinghouse ways, catering to hunters, people of the arts and visitors looking for peace and quiet up on the mountain.

Richmond House. Postcard circa 1905. At the top of the hill between North Settlement and Mitchell Hollow, along the Durham-Windham Turnpike (County Route 10), stands the very old Bennett Atwood Tavern, built around 1816. The Durham-Windham Turnpike ran from Prattsville through the northern part of Windham, over Mount Pisgah and connected with the Susquehanna Turnpike in West Durham. This was an early route for teamsters and drovers. By the 1860s David Richmond became the new owner of the tavern and hotel. This is the house where Francis Burns grew up. He later became the first African-American Methodist bishop in the country. In later years Jake Sebolt ran this property as a farm.

Windham Baseball Team. Photograph circa 1898. Left to right: (bottom row) Mr. Hienz, Bub Brisack, Benjamin Talmadge, Harry Brockett; (middle row) John Jenne, Keeler Cole, Lemuel Mott: (top row) Dawson Thorpe, Fred Woodvine, Wray France, George Davis.

Frank and Hazel Keller. Photograph circa 1915. Big brother giving his little sister a friendly ride! Frank and his sister Hazel lived on Main Street just up Creamery Hill. Frank grew up to be a painter, paper hanger and custodian for the Methodist Church and Sunday school. Frank also ran his boyhood home as a boardinghouse, known as Keller's Cottage.

South Street Looking East through Windham Valley. Glass plate, circa 1890. The old turnpike (Route 23) runs east to west in the center of the photograph. The wooden bridge lower left is crossing the Batavia Kill on the west end of South Street. Notice how narrow the creek was back then.

In the center of the photograph is another wooden bridge crossing the Batavia Kill, today near the home of Linda Rusk. Many of the buildings on the right were part of Jared Matthew's farm. Later it was the site of his shaving box, button mold and broom handle factories. His son Levi continued to run the family business until 1883. By the mid-1920s the farm belonged to George Muller. Later, George constructed a creamery building out of bricks. It is now Guricki's Windham Auto Body Shop.

Ladies by the Stream. Photograph circa 1905. These fine-looking ladies are obviously enjoying the beautiful outdoors and the stream here in Windham. There is yet another picture of these same ladies with their bicycles. Some are wearing identical uniforms and the same flat hats. These ladies are most likely visiting from a private school, or just making a fashion statement.

The lady third from the right is Jane Graham, wife of Harry Brockett and grandmother of Mary Brockett Holcomb.

Windham House AND Cottage,

WIMDHAM, (IN THE CATSKILLS,) N. Y.

First-class Boarding House with large, well furnished rooms, and has ample accommodations for 60 guests. Bath. Toilet. Good spring water. Table supplied with fresh milk, eggs and vegetables from Farm connected with House. Two New York mails daily.

No Hebrews Taken. Write for Booklets.

C. R. SANFORD & SON, Prop'rs.

The Windham House. Photograph circa 1895. The most wonderful thing to consider about this beautiful old photograph of an historic landmark on the old turnpike is that the hotel is still in operation.

In 1795 Perez Steele and family came to Windham from Connecticut. After a time Steele purchased this large farm. By 1805 a large farmhouse was built to accommodate his family of six children. This was the Steele Homestead. By 1836 Perez's son, Colonel Stephen Steele, purchased the farm. Stephen immediately enlarged it and transformed the farmhouse into a traveler's "tavern and drover's inn." He also acquired the contract to be the headquarters for the Catskill and Delhi stage line, serving a large area of the mountaintop.

Sometime after Colonel Steele retired, the inn was purchased by Sherman Munger, circa 1867. He further enlarged the building and added six large pillars and railing, creating a very distinctive-looking boardinghouse and resort, newly named The Windham House.

In 1911 Mr. and Mrs. Caleb Sanford bought the boardinghouse and ran it for forty years. It was sold to the present owners, Stanley and Roberta Christman, in 1951. Along with their son Brian and his wife Ruth, the Christman family has developed one of the most beautiful resorts on the mountaintop.

South Street

Windham Country Club. Photograph circa 1930. To keep up with the times and the changing activities of tourists to Windham, it was decided by local hotel and business owners that a golf course was needed. In 1927 they selected approximately seventy-five acres of open pastureland along South Street on which to build the course. In 1928 the new nine-hole golf course opened, becoming an integral part of attracting visitors to the summer boarding business on the mountaintop. In the early 1960s a second nine holes were added to accommodate the growing interest in golf.

The Westmere. Photograph circa 1920. The Westmere was located at the eastern end of South Street across from the golf course on land owned by the Munson family. Silas Munson enlarged a small cottage on his property in the early 1880s to enable his son Alvah and Alvah's wife Elsie to establish their own boardinghouse in 1884. Alvah passed away five years later and left Elsie to manage the boardinghouse on her own, which she then called Elsie's Cottage. Elsie and her good friend Carrie West managed the hotel for many years. Then it was run by Carrie, her husband Nicholas and her daughter Anita, and they renamed the hotel The Westmere again. Anita's sister Nellie and her husband Milton Dunham bought The Westmere in 1924 and ran it for seventeen more years. There were several owners after that, until 1970 when James P. O'Connor purchased the property and it became known as the Windham Mountain Inn.

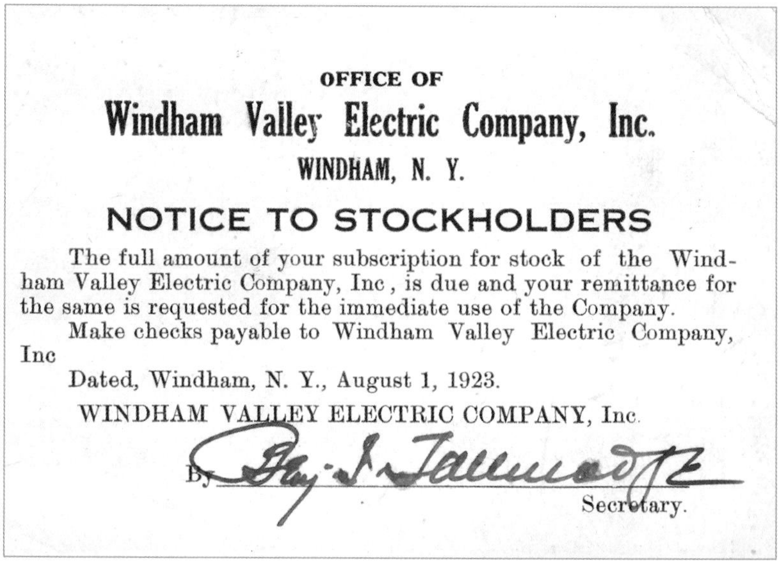
OFFICE OF

Windham Valley Electric Company, Inc.

WINDHAM, N. Y.

NOTICE TO STOCKHOLDERS

The full amount of your subscription for stock of the Windham Valley Electric Company, Inc, is due and your remittance for the same is requested for the immediate use of the Company.

Make checks payable to Windham Valley Electric Company, Inc

Dated, Windham, N. Y., August 1, 1923.

WINDHAM VALLEY ELECTRIC COMPANY, Inc.

By Ray. J. Tallmadge

Secretary.

First Air Mail. Photograph circa 1938. Windham Journal, *July 1930: "George W. Osborn has arranged for an airport on the Osborn House grounds near the Country Club House on South Street. Windham residents, visitors and guests will now have the opportunity of seeing the town from the air each Thursday and Friday. Also able to witness parachute jumping, stunts, air novelties, bombing, a human body hurled one thousand feet through the air and death defying spectacles. Holger Hoiries is to be the pilot and Tom Gibbons the jumper. Quite the novelty for the time in Windham." By 1938, to commemorate the twentieth anniversary of air mail service in the United States, Windham was selected as the first air mail pick-up site in Greene County. John Garraghan was the first pilot. Here we see Dennis Ferris, Windham postmaster, handing over the first bag of over a thousand pieces of mail to John Garraghan for his flight to Newark Airport.*

The Munson House. Photograph circa 1885. Another pioneer family, Solomon and Jarius Munson, moved to North Settlement in 1799 from Connecticut, settling the area around Batavia. Jarius's son Lemuel moved to the village of Windham and built his homestead on South Street. Lemuel farmed the flat fields all his life. As he got older, his son Silas and family moved back to the homestead and began taking in boarders around 1872.

The Munson House by 1900. Photograph circa 1900. As the building grew larger and larger, the Munson House could accommodate over one hundred guests. Silas Munson's son Lewis continued enlarging the hotel to its present size. The hotel changed hands several times within the family. The last owners were Chilton Munson Cammer and his wife Christine, who continued the family boardinghouse business tradition for another thirteen years.

Glass plate, circa 1898. Upon planning for their retirement, Silas and Phebe Munson built this beautiful Victorian house on the corner of Church and South Street in 1895. It is certainly the most photographed house in Windham. This house was passed down through the Munson family until Donald Fuller Munson and his wife Florence made it their home. After a time they began taking in boarders, as was the long family tradition. They named their house The Elmcrest Inn. Upon Donald's demise the house was eventually sold to buyers outside of the family.

Windham Village. Photograph circa 1906. In this beautiful picture taken from South Mountain looking north over Windham Village, you'll notice that most of the land has been turned into pastures and crop fields owing to the removal of the great hemlock forests for use in the tanning industry. Church Street is center-right foreground near the bottom, with Silas Munson's house on the northeast corner of South Street. Elmer Munson's Crest Park is left center. The Centre Church steeple is to the left on Main Street. The road heading north on the right is Mill Street. The large house with porch to the right of Mill Street center is A.E. West's The Glen House.

In the Catskill Mountains.
NEW PLANT
CREST PARK
MODERN
E. E. MUNSON, Proprietor.
Acetylene Light, thorough Sanitary System, Plumbing, Drainage, Bath, Toilet Room, etc.
Accommodates 50 Guests. No Hebrews.
WINDHAM, - GREENE CO., - NEW YORK.

Crest Park. Photograph circa 1930. In 1900 Elmer Munson, eldest son of Silas Munson, wanted to run his own boardinghouse. At the top of Church Street, Elmer built a large boardinghouse that he called Crest Park. Over the forty years that Elmer and his family ran Crest Park, he added sixteen additional buildings on the eleven-acre property. By 1940 the boardinghouse could accommodate 100–150 guests. As Elmer and his wife Rose were thinking about retiring, their youngest daughter Harriet and her husband Bill Davis moved back to Crest Park and eventually took over the business. Bill and his family of seven children ran the business until 1959, when it was sold and ceased operating as a boardinghouse.

Elmer Munson. Photograph circa 1908. Here we find Elmer with part of his large family that would help with the many aspects of running a boarding-house in future years. That's Elmer "Hum" Munson, about two years old, on his lap, along with his sister Margaret. Margaret went on to become a school teacher in Windham and Cairo. "Hum" became superintendent of maintenance at Bethlehem Central School.

Munson's Bridge. Photograph circa 1895. This picture finds us standing on the future site of Crest Park. Looking east over the Batavia Creek and Windham Village, we see a beautiful wooden bridge that crossed the creek along Church Street. There were several bridges before this one, starting in the 1850s. These bridges were each known as Munson's Bridge, as they led the way up the steep curving hill of Church Street to South Street, where the Munson families resided. It wasn't long after this picture was taken that this bridge was washed away in one of the many floods that assaulted the Windham valley. A new, two-bay iron bridge would soon replace it. That one lasted for sixty years before it was swept away during a major flood in 1960.

Brainerd Farm. Postcard circa 1915. Sometime around 1786 George Stimpson, the first settler in Windham, sold this farmland of 180 acres to Josiah Brainerd. For three generations the Brainerd family farmed the land. Josiah's grandson Cyril inherited the farm in 1880 and began taking in boarders. Over the years the resort grew to accommodate approximately eighty guests. Attending to their every need was Cyril's son Elbert and his daughter Eva. The Brainerds kept up the family business until 1957, when Wilhelm and Erna Goettsche purchased the resort. After about seven years of operation, the resort was sold to Kenneth O'Conner. O'Connor's large family of fourteen children made good use of the large house.

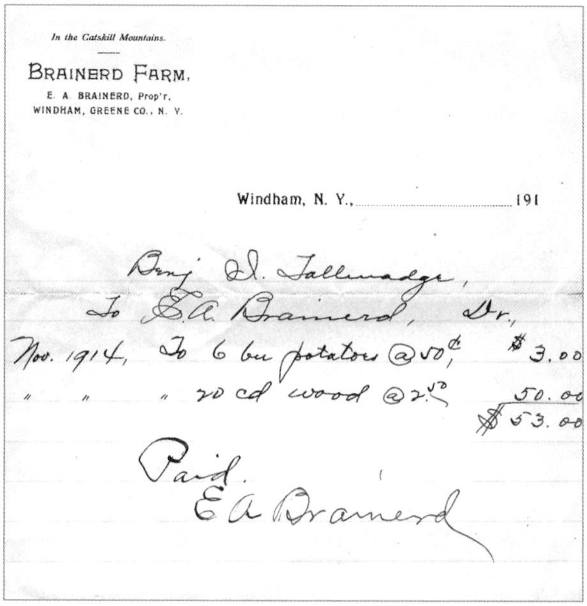

In the Catskill Mountains.

BRAINERD FARM,
E. A. BRAINERD, Prop'r,
WINDHAM, GREENE CO., N. Y.

Windham, N. Y., ... 191

Benj. D. Tallmadge,
To E. A. Brainerd, Dr.,

Nov. 1914,	To 6 bu potatoes @ 50¢,	$3.00
" "	" 20 cd wood @ 2.50	50.00
		$53.00

Paid.
E A Brainerd

The Brainerd Family. Photograph circa 1899. Three generations of the Brainerd family stand in front of the family boardinghouse on South Street.

Left to right: (adults) Elbert Brainerd (father of Eva and Edna), Olive Brainerd (mother of Eva and Edna), Cyril Brainerd, Sara Brainerd (wife of Cyril), William Brainerd, Virginia (wife of William); (little girls) Edna Brainerd (Eva's sister), Benetta Brainerd (William's daughter).

Eva Brainerd Moore. Photograph circa 1908. This picture speaks for itself.

1868.

A good wife is one who puts her husband in at the side of the bed next to the wall, and tucks him in to keep him warm in the winter, splits the wood, makes the fire in the morning, washes her husband's face and draws on his boots for him, never scolds, never suffers a rent to remain in her husband's small clothes, keeps her shoes up at the heel, and her stockings darned, never wonders what her husband sees interesting in the young woman who lives across the way, never slams the door loud when her husband is speaking, and always reproves the children when they eat up their father's supper.

Red Falls

As we cross over the town line of Ashland on our way to Prattsville, we first come to the hamlet of Red Falls. Not unlike the village of Prattsville, Red Falls owes its existence to one family—the Morsses. Forster Morss and his young family lived in Ashland village in 1800. He was busy with his tannery and gristmill on White Brook near Sutton Hollow Road for over twenty-five years.

In 1825 Forster and his son Burton moved to Federal City, later renamed Red Falls by Burton for the red sandstone that stained the Batavia Kill. The Morsses built a new and larger tannery in Red Falls, employing about fifty workers. The tanneries were very successful. Over the next twenty years a gristmill was built, along with a sawmill, shingle mill, cider mill, distillery and cotton mill. A foundry was built, indispensible in forging all of the machinery necessary for operating the mills and other industries.

The hamlet of Red Falls had its own school, post office, store, creamery and many cottages that Burton built for his workers.

Village View. Photograph circa 1896, De Lisser, Picturesque Catskills. *In this photograph almost all of the industry is now gone, with only a few businesses left to help sustain life in this once-thriving community.*

Photograph circa 1895. In the mid-1800s many Irish families emigrated from New England to the western part of Greene County to work in Burton's enterprises in Red Falls. Burton was very good to his workers, and they raised large, hard-working families. Burton believed education was very important for his workers, so he built them this fine school at the bottom of Red Falls Road. Although the industries in Red Falls declined near the end of the 1800s, these children still look like their families are prospering.

Photograph circa 1910. As the Batavia Kill nears Red Falls, the creek bed becomes quite wide, with many opportunities to harness the power of the water to run the mills along the creek.

MAY 1895.

On Friday last we wiggled away from our editorial duties, and started for Prattsville. It may be a relief to the community to know that we passed over the miserable roads between Ashland and Prattsville, with a whole neck. By the way that road near Red Falls is a disgrace to civilization and we are glad to learn that a new road will be laid out over the premises of M. Benham Martin.

Photograph circa 1898. These very substantial stone abutments seem to be holding up a primitive wooden bridge crossing the Batavia Kill just below the falls and cotton mill. Many roads were needed to service all the mills on both sides of the Batavia Kill. Today there is virtually no evidence remaining of any of the mills at the falls site.

Photograph circa 1895. Looking east over Red Falls, the Windham Turnpike (Route 23) is on the left. The large white building is one of several mills and factories operating in the hamlet. The very large building in the rear, center of photograph, was earlier the cotton mill. As the tanning industry declined in the late 1840s, Burton Morss went into the cloth industry. In 1848 Burton built this large building, 50' by 100' and three and one half stories tall. The mill operated with two turbine overshot waterwheels. Eighty employees operated some seventy looms for weaving yard-wide sheeting; other machinery was used for making cotton yarn, wraps, wicking twines and batts.

Many of the workers were Irish immigrants, and Burton provided housing for them and for all his other workers who could not afford their own housing when they first arrived in Red Falls. Burton built for them a beautiful Catholic chapel in the mid-1840s—St. Joseph's Chapel—and it is still in use today.

The cotton mill was kept in operation until 1880 when the machinery became worn and the water flow unreliable. Some buildings were then used for the manufacture of carriages, sleighs and wagons. The main building was used for a chair factory or woolen mill.

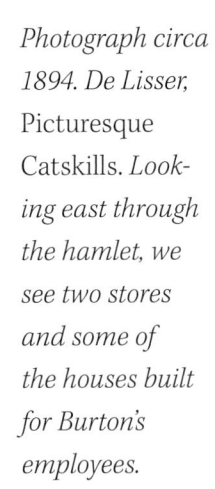

Photograph circa 1894. De Lisser, Picturesque Catskills. *Looking east through the hamlet, we see two stores and some of the houses built for Burton's employees.*

Photograph circa 1896. De Lisser, Picturesque Catskills. *This handsome structure, built by Burton Morss, was the dry goods store of William Wescott. The telegraph office and post office were also located here. By 1904, with the population decreasing, the post office was closed and moved to the village of Prattsville.*

Photograph circa 1895. Pictured is one of the sawmills needed to provide lumber for the Morsses' many business enterprises.

Photograph circa 1896. In the background is Irving Crane's blacksmith shop. On the road is a horse-drawn taxi giving tourists a ride to Prattsville.

Photograph circa 1898. In 1891 Irving Crane and his family moved from East Windham to Red Falls to begin blacksmithing. Crane occupied one of the larger early houses built by Burton. Notice the picket fence used to keep farm animals from roaming up to the house.

Photograph circa 1898. Another small house and store on Main Street.

October 1872.

Red Falls—the quiet little place, has been the scene of another outrage. On Friday week a number of women became engaged in a "war of words" which soon culminated in a sanquineous conflict in which brooms, stones, bricks and various other offensive and defensive weapons were brought in requisition.

Photograph circa 1910. This big, impressive house is without a doubt the home of Burton Morss and his son Burton Jr. In earlier years, circa 1895, this was the home of William Wescott. The house remains in beautiful condition today and is a lasting testament to the once-prosperous hamlet of Red Falls.

ASHLAND

Just five miles west of Windham, we come to the bustling village of Ashland. Most of the township's 900 inhabitants live in and around the village. In this panoramic view looking southwest over the village, there seem to be even fewer trees than we saw in Windham, owing to the tanning industry. The businesses along Main Street provide almost everything needed to live in this very rural community. Among the many enterprises in the late 1800s were two hotels, a doctor, shoemaker, cooperage, turning works cigar factory, two mercantile stores and three large hat-making factories.

The village school in 1882 taught 89 young scholars. Families were large in the mid-1800s, as it took many hands to run family businesses, homes and farms. In 1882 there were close to 900 children attending schools in Ashland, Windham and Prattsville.

Bird's-eye View of Ashland. Postcard circa 1913. Looking west through the Batavia Valley, one can see the village of Ashland from one end to the other. Left center is the Methodist Church. The road going off to the right is West Settlement Road. Right center is the Presbyterian Church.

One striking feature of this picture is the lack of trees on the mountains. When the first settlers arrived in the 1780s, the mountaintop was covered by a great hemlock forest. The trees were cut down for their bark, which was used in the tanning industry. By the 1850s the tanning industry declined rapidly because hemlock trees had become scarce. The former forest land was cleared, stone walls were built up and down the mountainside, and farming took over. Later, as farming went into its own decline, within a hundred years the forest reclaimed the land giving us the beautiful Catskills of our day.

When the first settlers came to the area around Ashland, they thought of themselves as better educated than most folks, so they named the village Scienceville. The name remained until 1848, when the growing township broke off from Old Windham and renamed itself Ashland, presumably after the potash works at the east end of the village.

As the first settlers were coming over from Durham to the Ashland region, they settled in five different locations—the Batavia Settlement (East Ashland), North Settlement, Sutton Hollow, Scienceville, and Richmond Four Corners.

The Batavia Settlement was the site of the first meetinghouse, raised in the fall of 1799, for all of Old Windham. It took many years to complete construction. The building served for town meetings and for church services for all denominations. It would later become the First Congregational Church of Old Windham, located on the present site of Pleasant Valley Cemetery. The North Settlement Methodist Church, built circa 1826, is still the oldest active church building on the mountaintop.

The region around Ashland today provides spectacular settings for many second homes built here over the last thirty years.

Sadly, there is only one remaining operating dairy farm on the mountaintop. The Valley View Farm in Ashland is lovingly run by Scott Tuttle and his wife Eve.

Photograph circa 1936. In the era before 1900, most children attended school at their nearby one-room schoolhouse and, yes, most students did walk to school. At that time an eighth-grade education was all that most students achieved. In 1900 the Windham Union School was built, teaching elementary and high school subjects. Many students from other towns attended the union school and boarded in town.

By the mid-1920s private bus service was already being provided by Frank Holdridge. In this picture we find Leslie Holdridge, Frank's son, with a bus he fashioned himself to take students to the Windham school. The bus is parked outside The Maples, where Leslie lived. The white building behind the bus is the home of Art and Jean Hamil, owners of Cave Mountain Motel.

The Maples. Photograph circa 1900. This very old stately homestead was built by Judge Levi Alden circa 1830. The main part of the house was constructed of bricks, a rare commodity on the mountaintop. Judge Alden was married to one of General Jehiel Tuttle's daughters. Tuttle owned the Drovers Tavern to the west.

Around 1922 the property was turned over to Frank Holdridge, who renovated the house and opened The Maples boardinghouse. Tragically, the house burned sometime in the early 1950s.

The two people on the left are Frank Bump and his wife, Lucy Holdridge Bump. Their son Harold is by the tree. The other gentleman is Albert Hoggens. Lucy was a half-sister of Frank Holdridge.

1860.

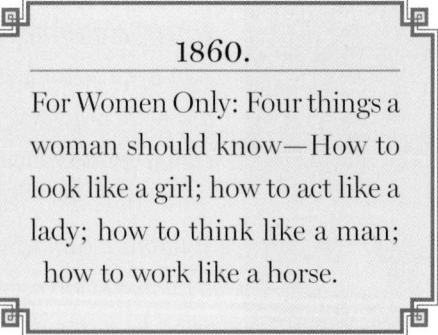

For Women Only: Four things a woman should know—How to look like a girl; how to act like a lady; how to think like a man; how to work like a horse.

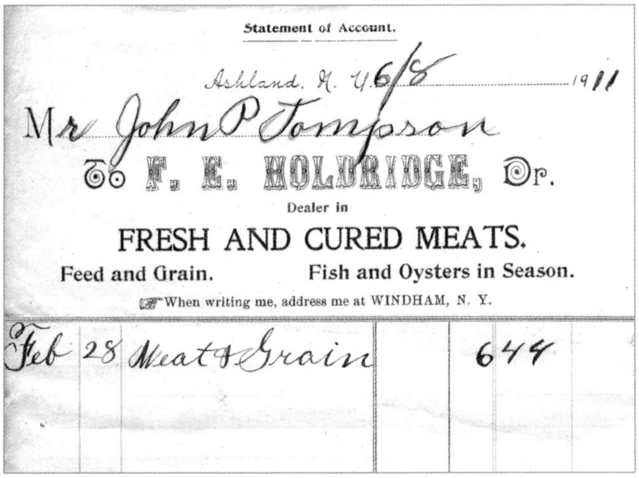
Statement of Account.

Ashland, N. Y. 6/8 1911

Mr John P Tompson

To F. E. HOLDRIDGE, Dr.

Dealer in

FRESH AND CURED MEATS.

Feed and Grain. Fish and Oysters in Season.

When writing me, address me at WINDHAM, N. Y.

Feb 28	Meat & Grain		6 44

The Bump House. Photograph circa 1951. This historic landmark was first known as The Traveler's and Drover's Hotel. It was situated along the Mohican Trail near the corner of Route 23 and North Settlement Road.

The hotel was most likely built by Captain Medad Hunt circa 1795 as a much-needed tavern to serve the many drovers and teamsters going to market. In its earliest years the tavern was run by Medad Hunt, and later turned over to his daughter Hannah and son-in-law General Jehiel Tuttle. The Tuttle records show that, for a time, Harry Steele's great-grandfather, Ephrim Bump, held the mortgage and it became necessary to foreclose on the tavern in 1830. This old tavern then became known as the Bump House.

In 1944 Harry Steele inherited the hotel and operated it for some time. Harry lived in the house across the road, and his wife ran the Heirloom Antiques Shop in the large barn.

In 1952 the Bump House was moved to the Farmer's Museum in Cooperstown by the L.I. Whipple moving company of Richfield Springs, New York. There it is on display today, fully restored as a monument to a time gone by in the Catskills.

Medad Hunt House. Photograph circa 1940. The year is 1780 and the Catskill Mountains are a wilderness. Along with other New Englanders comes Captain Medad Hunt down an old Indian trail from the north to the valley below known as the Batavia Settlement. Hunt purchased 500 acres, built a log cabin and developed a farm in this densely forested region. By 1792 Hunt was able to build this fine house from the trees he cleared off his land for pasture. As a road was developing east to west along the Batavia Kill, his house was also used as a tavern to serve the drovers. Hunt was instrumental in developing this small community along the Batavia Kill that was later to be known as Pleasant Valley. In later years this was a long-time residence of Bertram and Helen Lawrence and family.

Trinity Episcopal Church. Photograph circa 1900. The parish of Trinity Church was organized in 1799 by Reverend Philander Chase. After congregating in the Old Meeting House nearby for a number of years, in 1814 an Episcopal church was erected just west of Pleasant Valley Cemetery. Later the church suffered from serious neglect and was torn down. The present church was built in 1879. The bell from the Ashland Collegiate Institute hangs in the bell tower. Over the years the congregation became very small, the church closed, and the building is now a private business. Its beautiful exterior remains well maintained.

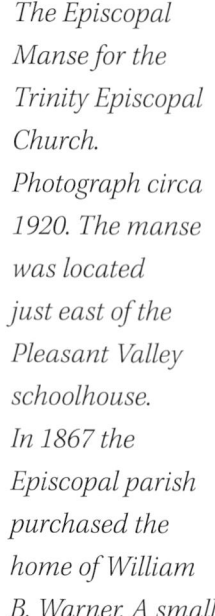

The Episcopal Manse for the Trinity Episcopal Church. Photograph circa 1920. The manse was located just east of the Pleasant Valley schoolhouse. In 1867 the Episcopal parish purchased the home of William B. Warner. A small house owned by Austin Smith was also purchased, moved to this site and added on to the Warner house to create the manse as pictured.

Around 1965 Ashland no longer had its own minister. The minister lived elsewhere and serviced many churches. The church then sold the manse to Ron and Audrey Gould. Later, Audrey married Frank Tompkins, who completely restored the house.

The Munger Homestead. Photograph circa 1908. This home is located just west of Pleasant Valley schoolhouse. Edward Munger was the first of five generations to live here. Edward's son, Sherman, was owner of the Windham House at one time. Edward's granddaughter Pauline married Clifford Lawrence and raised their family here. Cliff Lawrence and son "Larry" were in the excavating business for many years. Cliff and his brother Bert began a turkey farm business in 1963. Many will remember getting their Thanksgiving Day turkey at the Lawrence farm.

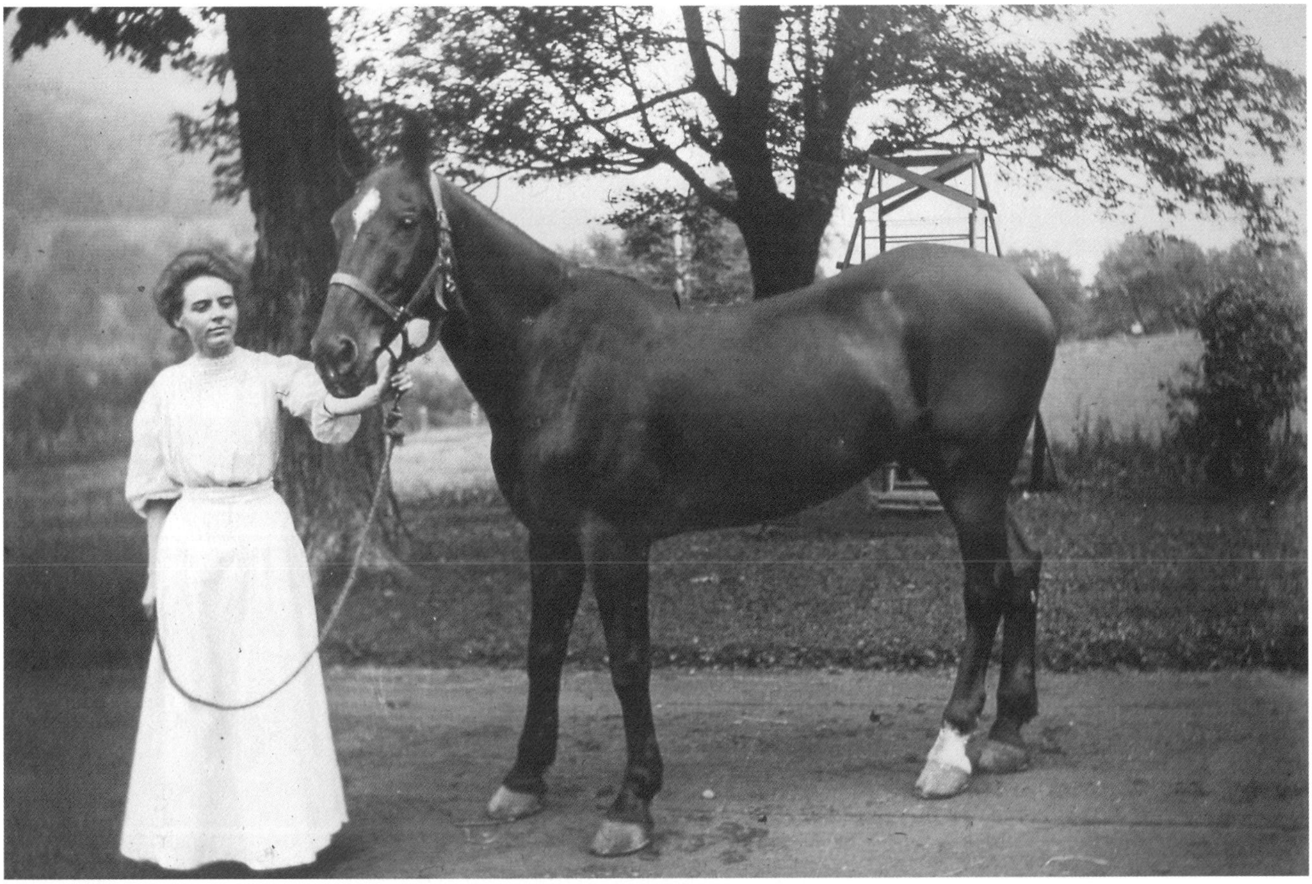

Photograph circa 1900. Zada Clarke Munger, wife of Sherman Munger, holds her beautiful horse Filex.

Pleasant Valley School. Photograph circa 1897. This is located just west of Jewett Heights Road on the Old Turnpike. The little boy in front on far left is Frank Holdridge. Other students include Eddie Wycoff, Montana Wycoff, Harry Steele (with hat, first row), and Bessie Wycoff.

May 1888.

An Ashland school Ma'am has introduced a new feature in her school. When one of the girls miss a word, the boy who spells it gets permission to kiss her. As a result the boys are improving rapidly

The Prout Homestead. Photograph circa 1890. John Prout, one of the very earliest pioneers of Windham, moved to Old Windham in 1799 and put down roots in the Batavia Settlement, one of the earliest settlements on the mountaintop. The house, built by Stephen Symmons, would become the Prout Homestead for many generations and was known as Elm Cottage. As you can tell by the photograph, the family was very prosperous. John's grandson, Reverend Henry Hedges Prout, wrote about the early beginnings of the Windham Township in the Windham Journal *from February 1869 to March 1870. "Old Times in Windham" is the oldest written, firsthand account, as Henry had the chance to speak with many of the original settlers and record their stories.*

In later years this homestead became Mayfair Farms, owned by Mr. Soccoza. Today it is the home of Dr. Jacquelyn Maier.

Photograph circa 1896. For a time I thought this old long-abandoned schoolhouse was the Prout District #2 Schoolhouse located on the northeast corner of the Prout Homestead. Delia Prout believes this to be the Pleasant Valley schoolhouse in District #3 (The Bump District), located east of the foot of North Settlement Road on the old D. Tuttle farm. For many years it was referred to as the "school under the elms."

Pleasant Valley Home. Postcard circa 1905. This was originally built as a public house around 1816 on the Old Turnpike, today the corner of Campbell Road and Route 23. In 1818 Dr. Jacob Benham, eldest son of Dr. Thomas Benham, purchased the house from Mr. Babcock. The Benham family lived here for several generations. Thomas Benham had emigrated from Columbia County in 1793. He made his professional visits on horseback for many years over a very large area and was happy when Dr. Hervey Camp moved to Windham circa 1814 to help share in the care of the early settlers.

Jacob Benham's daughter, Nancy Halcomb Benham (by his second wife, Clarissa Arnold), married Newell Snow. The Snow family lived here for several generations, and this was Mary Benham Snow Wooley's home.

In the early 1900s the Campbell family worked the boardinghouse and farm for the Snows, and Mary grew up with the Campbell children. The Campbell family took over the farm about 1926. In later years the farm was run by B.G. Partridge. The house is now gone.

Milk Pick-Up. Photograph circa 1905. Coming down Campbell Road and approaching Route 23, the old wooden milk can dock is opposite the Snow farmhouse. Campbell Road was not far from the village of Ashland creamery. The whole milk was brought to the creamery directly in these ten-gallon milk cans. Farmers could leave their milk cans at milk stations such as these to be picked up by a hired man from the creamery. Farmers farther up in the high valleys would take their milk to a nearby separating station to skim off the cream. The skimmed milk was sent back to the farm to feed it to the pigs. Most likely, the lads depicted are the two Campbell boys waiting for the milk wagon.

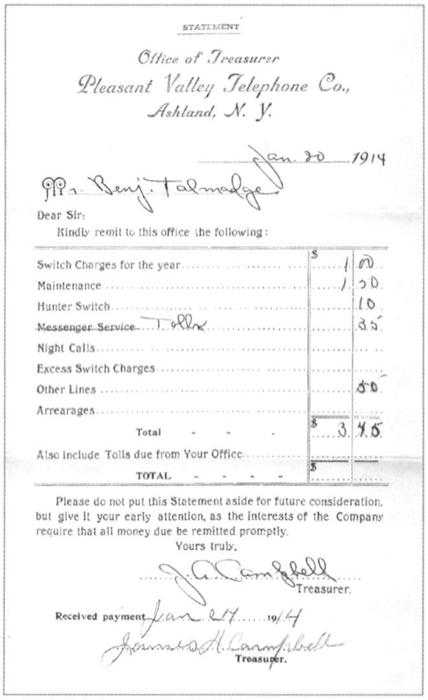
STATEMENT

Office of Treasurer
Pleasant Valley Telephone Co.,
Ashland, N. Y.

Jan. 20 1914

Mr. Benj. Talmadge

Dear Sir:
Kindly remit to this office the following:

Switch Charges for the year	$ 1.00
Maintenance	1.50
Hunter Switch	.10
~~Messenger Service~~ Tolls	.35
Night Calls	
Excess Switch Charges	
Other Lines	.50
Arrearages	
Total	$ 3.45
Also include Tolls due from Your Office	
TOTAL	$

Please do not put this Statement aside for future consideration, but give it your early attention, as the interests of the Company require that all money due be remitted promptly.

Yours truly,
J. C. Campbell
Treasurer.

Received payment Jan. 27 1914
James H. Campbell
Treasurer.

Photograph circa 1906. Here we find James Campbell performing the weekly chore of making butter in the old butter churn. This photograph was taken at the Snow farm on Campbell Road.

The White Homestead. Photograph circa 1900. On this site, just east of Sutton Hollow Road, in 1784 Elisha Strong built one of the first log cabins in the area and moved his family here from Connecticut in 1785. Strong's eldest daughter married Deacon Argulus White, who settled on the Strong homestead in 1793. Sometime later White erected this house, which still stands today. It was Elmer Roe's home in later years and was called the Maple Shade House.

Photograph circa 1891. I think I can still smell the paint drying on this brand new bridge on the old turnpike at the foot of Sutton Hollow Road. This finely dressed lady is obviously inspecting the fine workmanship on this bridge, one of the first iron ones in Ashland.

Looking West along Main Street around 1900. Photograph circa 1900. On the right, the first building center is Sommer Lee's Store. The next building west is the Ashland Centre Hotel.

Hat Factory. Photograph circa 1880. At one time in the 1850s, there were three hat factories in the village of Ashland. One factory was that of Strong and Ruggles, located between Hattie Munson's house and the Dodge Brothers Garage. This factory, along with the shoe shop of Mr. Halsted, the Harness Shop of Dumah Tuttle, and the Packing Box Shop behind the hat factory, were destroyed by fire in 1858.

Near West Settlement Road was the hat factory of Conine and Tompkins, and near Sutton Hollow Road, on the south side, was the Hat Shop, pictured, of White and Winne.

MAY 1870.

There seems to be an unusual scarcity of girls in this section. We mean girls who are not afraid to WORK for a living, not the fastidious young damsels who sit primed up and powdered in the parlor, while their mothers do the work … . Why is it that girls who love work are becoming so scarce? Would it not be better for many if instead of aspiring to be a "school-marm" or a music teacher, they would go out in the dairy where health and genuine beauty are in store for them—and go to work? What sight is more pleasing than to see the buxom farmer's daughter, her cheeks glowing with health, and her hair hanging in bewitching carelessness down her pearly neck and over her shoulders, trip gaily out to the cow yard at milking time and sit fearlessly down by the side of "Old Red" and with her dainty fingers gently press the lacteal fluid from the yielding udder?

Sommer Lee's Grocery Store. Photograph circa 1905. As early as 1860 Egbert Dodge was engaged in the grocery business at this location. Some years later Sommer Lee, from an old family in Ashland, took over the dry goods business and operated it for many years. In the early 1920s, silent movies were shown upstairs over the store. In 1921 Ralph Rhinehart took over Lee's store and added a full line of groceries. In 1947 Demerest Farm Stores remodeled this building and opened a branch store with Walter Pelham as manager.

Sommer Lee's Store. Photograph circa 1916. Inside the store we find Barton Gordon and Homer Tompkins putting up a new wainscot ceiling. Sommer, of course, is supervising the fine work. Notice the wood parlor stove used for heat.

Ashland Centre Hotel. Photograph circa 1900. An old Ashland landmark, this hotel was first built as a public house. Public houses were very similar to the drover's hotels, but on a smaller scale. By 1859 this was the only public house in the village. Later owners were C.L. Berry in 1863 and Mr. Mattice in 1891. For a number of years around 1920, Vernon Ferris kept the hotel and also opened a large room (Ferris' Hall) for dances and other entertainment. In 1933 Ferris opened a grocery store across the road (IGA store).

October 1887.

The telegraph is working to Ashland. The office is in Lee's store. Will is puzzling over the dots and dashes.

Ashland Methodist Church. Photograph circa 1910. The Methodist Church of Old Windham and Ashland met for over forty years in the Old Meeting House and in the village schoolhouses. The Methodists shared these places of worship with the Presbyterians for many years, and also with the Episcopalians for a time. This at times led to strained relationships. In 1843 the Methodists left the Old Meeting House and built their own churches in Ashland and Windham Village.

In 1935 the Methodist and Presbyterian churches in Ashland merged, using the Presbyterian Church for services. In later years the Methodist Church was taken down.

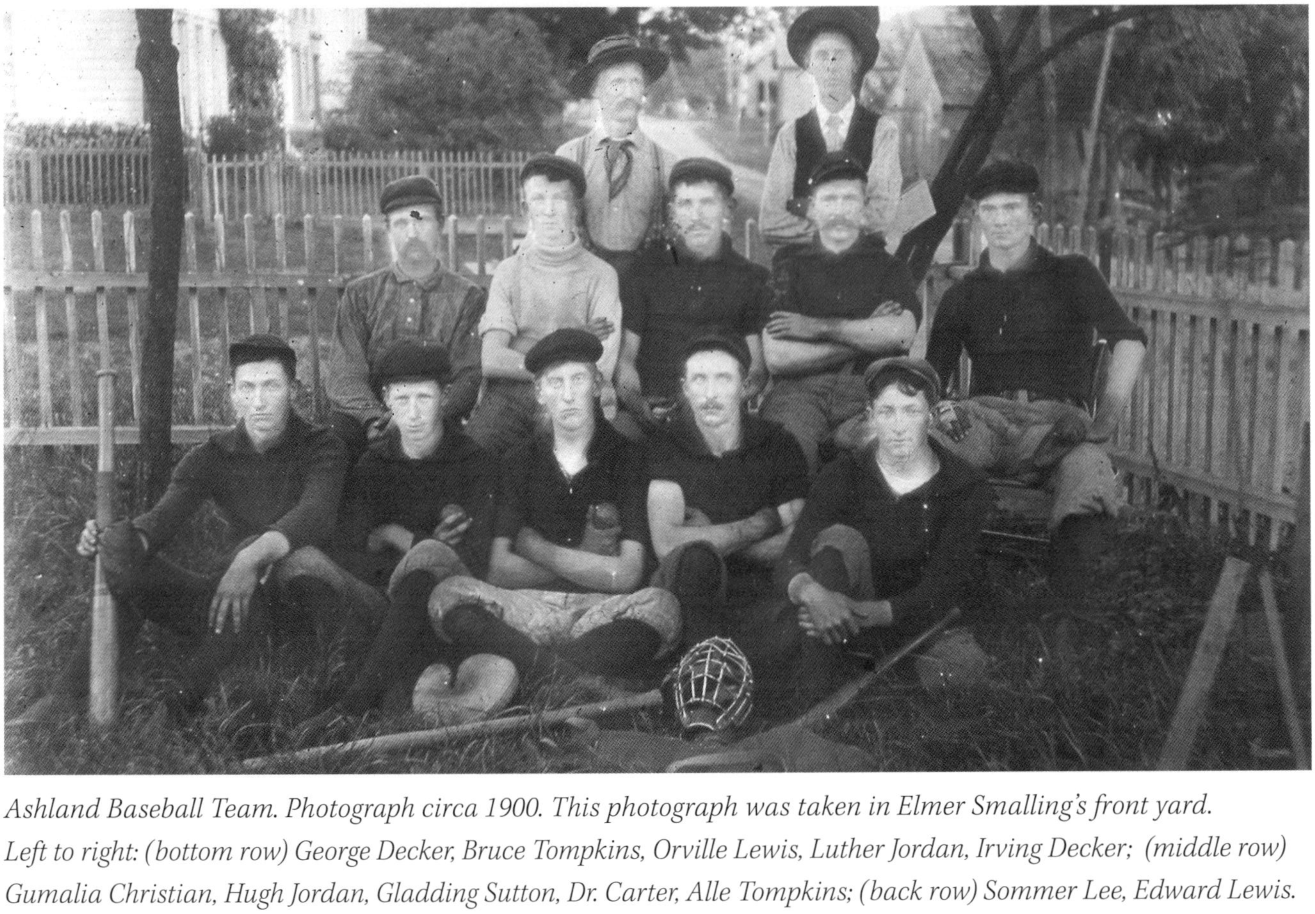

Ashland Baseball Team. Photograph circa 1900. This photograph was taken in Elmer Smalling's front yard. Left to right: (bottom row) George Decker, Bruce Tompkins, Orville Lewis, Luther Jordan, Irving Decker; (middle row) Gumalia Christian, Hugh Jordan, Gladding Sutton, Dr. Carter, Alle Tompkins; (back row) Sommer Lee, Edward Lewis.

Ashland Creamery. Photograph circa 1910. The Township of Ashland had a large community of farmers. Making butter for one's own family with an old wooden churn was one thing, but making butter and cheese from thirty or forty cows to help support the family was quite another. The community needed a far more extensive enterprise. In 1872 Austine Smith, a farm owner with eighty cows, built on the Batavia Kill what is most likely the first creamery in Ashland. He was using the milk from about 225 cows and considered his venture a profitable investment. By 1890, milk from 500 cows was processed at the creamery, with Daniel Steele as the butter maker. The creamery was rebuilt about 1902, as pictured. It ceased operation around 1935.

Elmer Smalling House. Photograph circa 1895. This very old house next to the Methodist Church was occupied by the C.W. Smalling family in 1856. A son, Elmer Smalling, also raised his family here. Elmer was the town photographer. The little building on the left that looks like a caboose was his studio. In the early 1980s this became the home of Ted and Alice Smith. Now it is the home of Scott Schoonmaker.

Ashland Collegiate Institute and Musical Academy. Drawing, circa 1860. This two-year boarding school with college academic standing was first organized as The Hedding Literary Institute in 1854. The course of study centered on music, art, language, and engineering. There were four quarter-terms each year. Room and board and tuition were all-inclusive, and the cost was about $36 per term. Students came from a 150-mile radius to attend the "Seminary," as it was called.

In 1856 the school was forced to reorganize as the Ashland Collegiate Institute. While the college was never officially under the control of the Methodist Church, it was closely affiliated with that religious denomination. The college continued for another five years until 1861, when a fire burned it to the ground, never to be rebuilt.

F.L. Dodge Store. Photograph circa 1910. This building was originally the home of Dr. P.I. Stanley in the 1860s. Egbert Dodge opened his first store before moving to this location around 1882. Egbert, his son F.L. Dodge, and grandson Fred Dodge ran this store and post office for over seventy years. In 1956 the site was sold to Mr. Guida, later to become the Landmark restaurant. It was last run as a restaurant in the 1970s by Eugene McKillop.

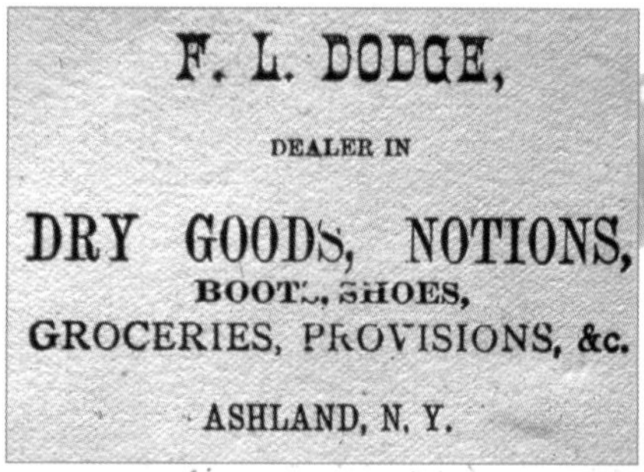

F. L. DODGE,

DEALER IN

DRY GOODS, NOTIONS,
BOOTS, SHOES,
GROCERIES, PROVISIONS, &c.

ASHLAND, N. Y.

A.B. Munson Store. Photograph circa 1915. Looking west on Main Street through Ashland, we see local residents out shopping. Munson sold dry goods and hardware. By the 1940s Roy Cornell operated a hardware store here. In 1950 Irving Winchell and family came to town, bought the business and sold hardware and farm equipment. By 1955 Irving was in the propane gas business, serving customers for many years until he retired. The structure is now an apartment building.

December 1921.

If you should notice people on the street with their heads held high, don't come to the conclusion that they are Presbyterians. They are probably watching the aeroplane.

Village Schoolhouse and Presbyterian Church. Postcard circa 1909. Nearly across from Munson's store is the Village Schoolhouse, District #1. This was the second schoolhouse in the village, the first one being made of logs on Argulas White's property near the corner of Sutton Hollow Road and the Old Turnpike. That school burned down around 1820. The second building remained in use until the schools were centralized, at which time most one-room schoolhouses were sold for as little as one dollar. Today it is a private home.

Stewart Tuttle is the teacher, on the left.

The Presbyterian Society was organized in 1802 and met at the Old Meeting House at the Batavia Settlement. The Presbyterians left the Batavia Meeting House and established a church in 1843 in Scienceville, to the west, later to become Ashland Village in 1848. By the early 1930s, with dwindling membership in the Methodist and Presbyterian churches, they combined into a Community Church and used the Presbyterian Church for worship. The Methodist Church was eventually torn down and the Presbyterian Church was demolished by fire in the late 1960s, to be replaced by the present church.

Crescent Lawn. Photograph circa 1910. When first built as a parsonage for the Presbyterian Church in 1856, this was a much smaller building.

In 1859 Tom Jerald had finished his studies at the Ashland Collegiate Institute and went into the mercantile business with George Fox. Jerald married Frances Tuttle, the daughter of Albert Tuttle, in 1860. He and Frances moved back to Connecticut to pursue his business there.

In 1868 Albert Tuttle purchased the parsonage and the Strong residence to the west. There the Tuttles resided for some thirty years. In late 1898, Tom Jerald inherited the old parsonage and Strong house. Tom was now a very successful businessman with a large farm and several stores. He also had made fireworks at one time.

When Tom acquired the property, he renamed it Crescent Lawn. He made many additions and refinements to the old house, and it became the finest home in Ashland. By 1921 Tom's grandson Chester inherited the property. Chester sold the brick house and converted the Jerald Dairy Farm into a large chicken farm. The farm was in the Jerald family until 1969. Chester's estate was valued at $350,000 when he passed away.

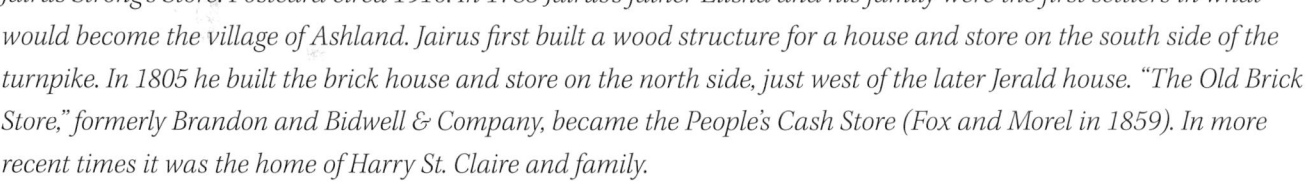

Jairus Strong's Store. Postcard circa 1910. In 1785 Jairus's father Elisha and his family were the first settlers in what would become the village of Ashland. Jairus first built a wood structure for a house and store on the south side of the turnpike. In 1805 he built the brick house and store on the north side, just west of the later Jerald house. "The Old Brick Store," formerly Brandon and Bidwell & Company, became the People's Cash Store (Fox and Morel in 1859). In more recent times it was the home of Harry St. Claire and family.

Ormsbee Tavern. Photograph circa 1920. Solomon Ormsbee and family settled in the village about 1787, near where the old tavern now stands. Sometime around 1805, Solomon built his tavern along the same lines as the Bump House and Windham House. By this time a new road had been laid out, upon which the present village stands. The tavern changed hands several times over the years. In 1864 Jonas M. Smith bought the tavern from W.P. Humphrey and renamed it the Ashland House. It has also been known as the Old Village Tavern. In 1925 Claude and Ethel Tompkins purchased the house and farm. It continues to be owned by the Tompkins family today.

Flora Dunham. Photograph circa 1903. This is Flora Dunham at about eighteen years of age. She was the daughter of Mr. and Mrs. Horace Dunham. Little did she know at that time that she would become one of the most beloved ladies of Ashland, held in the highest regard by her neighbors. Her husband, Robert "Bruce" Tompkins, was a lifelong farmer, while Flora tended her millinery shop. Her passion for the life and history of her community led her to be Ashland Town Historian as well as a correspondent for several Greene County newspapers. Flora was noted for her many beautiful hats.

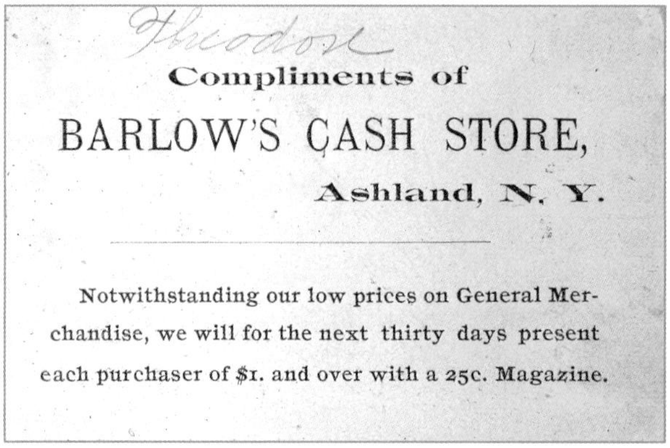

Compliments of

BARLOW'S CASH STORE,

Ashland, N. Y.

Notwithstanding our low prices on General Merchandise, we will for the next thirty days present each purchaser of $1. and over with a 25c. Magazine.

Florence Tompkins Conine. Photograph circa 1912. No one has ever said that life was easy living on a farm 100 years ago. At the Cornelius Tompkins farm on Steinmetz Road, carrying your share of work on the farm started at an early age. Here we see Florence Tompkins, five years old, working with a team of very large horses. Florence lived in North Settlement all her life, marrying Harold Conine in later years. They had one daughter, Diane.

Lambert Cooke Home. Photograph circa 1900. We are back in East Ashland and traveling up North Settlement Road. Halfway up we come to the Cooke farm. Lambert's son Claude and his grandson Tim carried on the farm for many years.

In 1867 this was the Marcus Fink farm. His daughter Christine married Ira Thompson and together they began the Thompson House in Windham.

North Settlement Separating Station. Photograph circa 1908. Just north of what was later Dick Daum's house was the milk station. In 1904 the milk station was taking in enough milk to produce 175 pounds of butter. In 1906 Marvin Mulford was in charge. Farmers too far from the Ashland Creamery could bring their milk to a station like this to be separated, leaving the cream to be made into butter and bringing the skimmed milk back home.

Dana and Jessie Mulford's Home. Photograph circa 1914. Dana and Jessie Mulford with their son Gerald at their home at the top of North Settlement Road. A second son, Elven, born a few years later, was the father of Gordon and George Mulford. Jessie died young. Dana and his second wife, Katherine, were the parents of Wesley Mulford. Dana was a farmer most of his life.

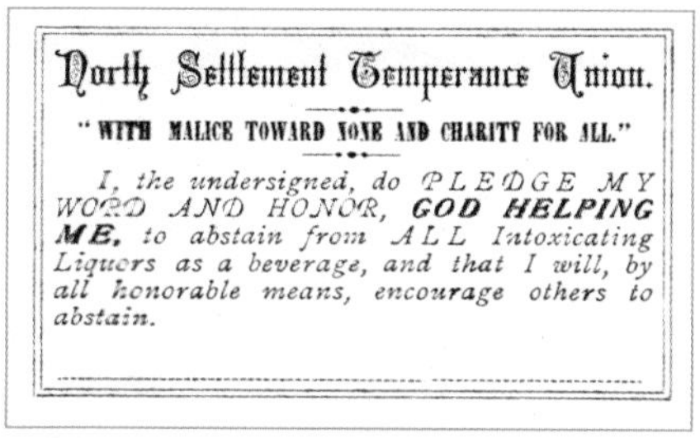

North Settlement Temperance Union.

"WITH MALICE TOWARD NONE AND CHARITY FOR ALL."

I, the undersigned, do PLEDGE MY WORD AND HONOR, **GOD HELPING ME**, to abstain from ALL Intoxicating Liquors as a beverage, and that I will, by all honorable means, encourage others to abstain.

Top of North Settlement Road. Photograph circa 1910. We are at the junction with County Route 10, which in 1785 was the Durham-Windham Turnpike coming over Mount Pisgah to Windham. When the early pioneers reached this point, there were only blaze marks on trees to lead them down to the valley of the Batavia and the first small settlement located there. The farm pictured is that of Charles Frayer. The Frayers are a well-established family in the North Settlement area, living there since about 1850. Charles's son, Enos O. Frayer, lived on an adjoining farm.

It is most likely that this was the old Rice place that operated as a hotel for some time. It is the present home of Mrs. Carlton Van Hoesen.

North Settlement Church. Photograph circa 1910. Located just east of Steinmetz Road on County Route 10.

Built in 1826, this would become the mission church for the Windham Methodist Charge. It is still an active church today, having one service a year in August.

Of special note is that this was the home church of Minister Francis Burns. Francis was an African-American who was "boarded out" to Bennett Atwood, a local farmer and tavern keeper, who raised Francis from eight years of age. Francis was drawn to the ministry as he grew older and eventually became the first African-American Methodist missionary bishop in the United States. He preached several sermons at the North Settlement Church, but served most of his ministry at a mission church in Liberia.

Henry Cooke Homestead. Photograph circa 1890. Located on Route 32C, just north of County Route 10. Henry Cooke is standing, front left. Notice the log watering trough and the pipe running from the house. In later years this was the farm of Winn and Helen Maben. The house is now gone.

May 1899.

Path Masters should see to it that the loose stones are removed from highways at once, as the law directs. A few fines for failure to do so would have a wholesome effect.

William Sutton Homestead. Photograph circa 1898. The Suttons were early settlers in Sutton Hollow, first arriving about 1840. Depicted is the second house. The first burned circa 1895. The house now belongs to John and Susan Eley, who have faithfully restored it.

Left to right: Irving Fuller; Emma Fuller, holding baby Harold; Grace Sutton, who lived her whole life here, holding baby Florence; Alice Sutton; Ella Sutton; Russell Sutton, father of Claude; Claude Sutton, father of Walter, Louise and Grace.

Sutton Hollow Schoolhouse. Photograph circa 1930. This schoolhouse is located just south of the Sutton homestead and is the last one-room schoolhouse on the mountaintop to remain just as it was when it closed circa 1940. When it was abandoned, Grace and Louise Sutton watched over the building for over forty years, keeping it safe. I can still see Grace's hunting rifle standing near the kitchen door, ready!

Recognizing that this schoolhouse should be preserved, and being on the Windham-Ashland-Jewett School District school board at the time, I asked Grace and Louise Sutton and Alfred Partridge if they would donate the property to the school district to be forever preserved. (Each family owned half of the school property.) They all graciously agreed to donate their interests in the property to the school district for one dollar each. A codicil was added to the new deed that states that the school district will maintain the one-room schoolhouse and grounds as is, and never sell the property or contents.

For many years Linda Hitchcock Varelas would faithfully bring her sixth-grade class to the schoolhouse to experience and learn about school life in the 1920s from the following former students of the Sutton Hollow school: Carl Lane, Alfred Partridge, Grace Sutton, Larry Lane, Calvin Partridge and Walter Sutton. Also in attendance was Elwood Hitchcock, who taught in a one-room schoolhouse and later became district school superintendent for the mountaintop.

Inside the Sutton Hollow Schoolhouse. Photograph circa 1986. This photograph shows the school as it was left in the 1940s. There was a cast-iron stove surrounded by a metal jacket (enclosure) in the corner. Against the front wall is one of the original school desks that sat three to four pupils. A writing surface protruded from the back of the bench. In 1912, sixteen new, up-to-date school desks were installed in the schoolhouse by Trustee Claude Sutton. There is also a melodeon and crank phonograph in the schoolhouse.

The building also served as a church in its earliest days, and the podium is still in the room. The rear door goes to the woodshed. There are two outhouses in the back.

1908 Class of Sutton Hollow School. Photograph 1908. Left to right: (first row) Lucy Ferris, Iva Clark, Albert Tompkins, Alice Sutton; (second row) Earl Partridge, Nettie Waterman, Florence Sutton, Georama Partridge, Grace Mabey, Katherine Lynch, Mable Clark, Louise Sutton, Leo Clark; (third row) Alice Ferris, Birdelle Weed.

The Waterman Homestead. Postcard circa 1906. Here is a classic photograph of life and the people who settled on the mountaintop. We find John and Adeline Tompkins Waterman and their son Manley J. at their homestead on County Route 10 just east of Partridge Road. They were one of the very earliest families to settle in Ashland, and farmed the land all their lives. The present Waterman Farm is less than a mile away and was one of the last dairy farms on the mountaintop.

Tuttle Homestead. Photograph circa 1882. This is a wonderful family portrait of the Burton Garfield Tuttle family. Burton, a relative of the first Tuttles to settle Old Windham in the 1790s, came to the West Settlement area of Ashland (at the top of West Settlement Road) and built this large farmhouse circa 1855. It proved necessary for the twelve children his wife bore him. Burton was obviously a very prosperous farmer. The house has been remodeled with an addition.

Today Scott Tuttle carries on the family tradition. Burton's great-grandson operates the last dairy farm on the mountaintop, in Pleasant Valley.

In this picture are: Burton and wife, Lacy Foot, sitting; their children Georgia Ann, Elven, Everette, Mary, Emma, Bertha, Ida, Eleanor, Alpheus, Laura. The two boys on the right are Irving, Howard Tuttle's father, and Dwight, Roberta Tuttle Zegal's grandfather.

The Clarke Homestead. Photograph circa 1898. In West Settlement on Ceila Tompkins Road. In this picture we find Viola Clarke holding Aletha, and Charles Clarke with their older daughter Zayda. George Clarke is with the dog. Zayda would grow up to become the wife of Sherman Munger, who owned and ran the Windham House.

December 1913.

The Pleasant Valley Telephone line has been connected to the switch board. Now we can talk to Prattsville and Windham.

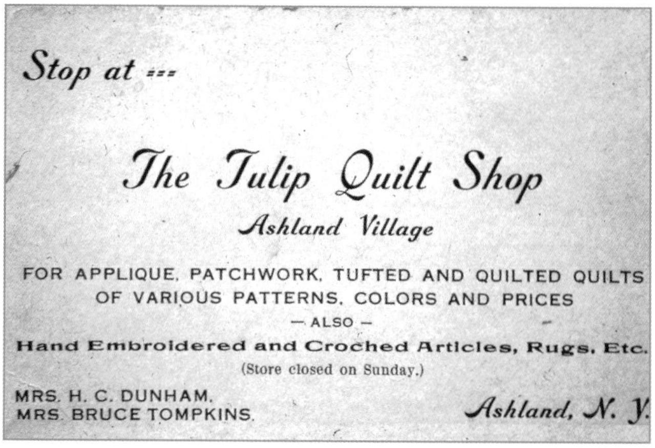

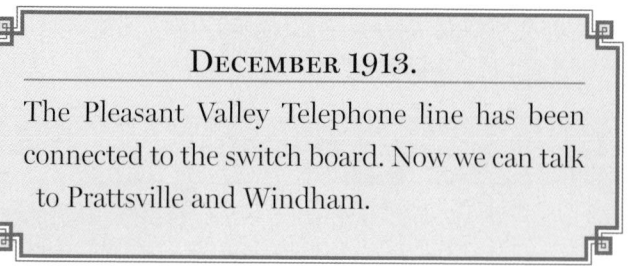

West Settlement Schoolhouse District #5. Photograph circa 1896. On County Route 10 just west of West Settlement Methodist Church. The school later became the home of Bruce Keller, then Chris Hellmer.

The teacher is Grace Adams. The students are (not in order): Tracy Tompkins, Walter Clark, Rice Tompkins, Myrtle Hummel, Maude Hummel, Mame Tompkins, Ralph Kurau, George Brezee, Howard Clark, S.B. Beers, Earl Tompkins, Edith Richmond, Jessie Griffin, Eva Tompkins, Ernest Christian, George (?), and Alice (?).

James Tompkins's Gravestone. Photograph circa 1980. West Settlement was the site of the homes of many early settlers in this part of Old Windham. Here, in this small cemetery in West Settlement, lie James Tompkins and his family. James, his wife and four children moved from Eastchester, New York, to this area in 1810. James had been a fifer in the Revolutionary War. Along with his family he farmed the land his whole life.

James is my great-great-great-great-grandfather. He was the first Tompkins to settle on the mountaintop, and therefore the patriarch of all the Tompkins descendents living on the mountaintop today. In 1810 he was already a sixth-generation American. His ancestor, Ralph, arrived in Boston on the ship True Love *in September 1636. Ralph's descendents helped settle a number of towns as they moved around New England.*

Today's descendents of James Tompkins, as well as the Tuttles, Hitchcocks, Brainerds, Osborns, Barlows and Munsons, to name but a few, should feel very proud of their ancestors and their accomplishments in settling the mountaintop and building our communities.

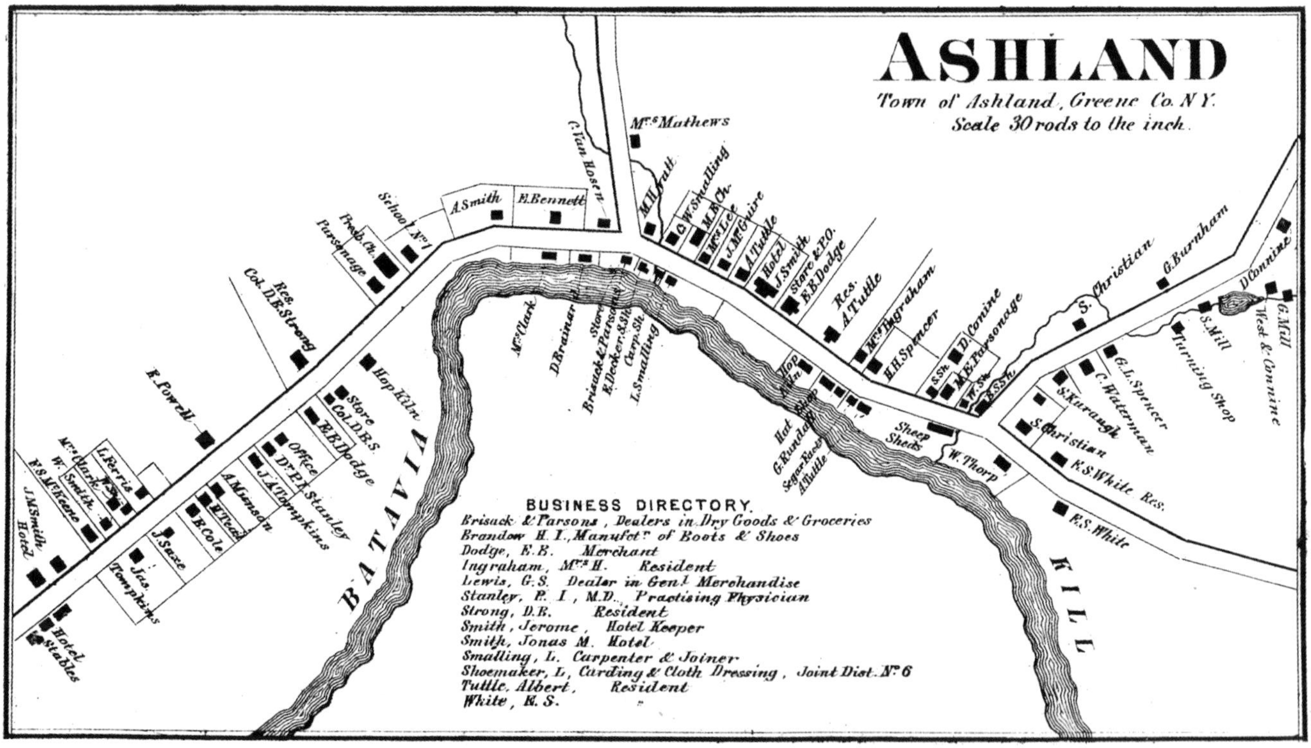

Main Street, Ashland, 1867.

Prattsville

The panorama on the next page, looking northeast over the village of Prattsville, again attests to the ravages of the tanning industry on the forests. There is a heavy concentration of homes and businesses on Main Street.

The Schoharie Kill drew men like Colonel Edwards to Hunter and Zadock Pratt to Prattsville, where they would harness the power of the stream to run the numerous industrial enterprises that began in the early 1800s, building prosperous villages in this vast wilderness of hemlock trees. Zadock Pratt first learned tanning as a boy with his father at Mill Hollow in Jewett. His driving ambition allowed him to make his first fortune in saddle making, furs and ash oars. With $14,000 in his pocket, he came to Schohariekill (the original name of the settlement) in 1824 to build the largest tannery in the world. A thriving and beautiful village was created in the process. Pratt helped build most of the early housing for his mill workers, and also the churches and other public buildings to attract professionals such as doctors and lawyers, and tradesmen such as printers and jewelers, in order to provide services for the expanding village population of over 1,500 inhabitants. Good farming practices instituted by Pratt provided the way for Prattsville to move forward after the tanning industry waned and disappeared.

Pratt was a very colorful man and was very proud of his accomplishments and what he had done to better the lives of his neighbors. He also worked for his country by serving two terms in the United States House of Representatives, helping to move this new country forward. The village of Schohariekill was set apart from Old Windham in 1833 and its name was changed to Prattsville in his honor.

Prominent buildings in this photo are the Prattsville Methodist Church in the right corner and the steeple of the Dutch Reformed Church in the extreme left corner. The two-story building with columns is the Prattsville Academy. Washington Street is winding its way up to County Route 10 in right center of the photo. In the lower foreground was the site of Pratt's tannery.

View of Prattsville. Photograph circa 1906.

Big Rock. Postcard circa 1910. As the Schoharie Kill Bridge and Toll Company pushed its way through dense forest westward past Windham and Ashland, little stood in its way until road workers reached the tiny settlement of Schohariekill (East Prattsville). There they encountered this huge rock near the confluence of the Batavia Kill and the Schoharie Kill. For over 120 years, for lack of resolve and dynamite, this landmark remained here. The rock provided ample photograph opportunities and a place on which to paint directions and advertising. When the road was rebuilt in the 1920s, the rock had to go.

In this photograph druggist Joseph Platner stands on top of the rock. We are looking east down Route 23. Just past the big rock going west was the Windham Turnpike Toll House.

The Schoharie Kill Valley Fairgrounds. Postcard circa 1908. By 1882 Prattsville had become a large farming community. The tanning industry had ended here by 1860 because of the depletion of hemlock trees. In 1882 local farmers banded together to established the Prattsville Agricultural and Horticulture Association. Every year the association held an agricultural fair across the turnpike from the Big Rock to demonstrate their successes in crop growing, animal husbandry, cooking and horticulture. There was a racetrack for trotters that circled the fairgrounds. Another highlight was a hot-air balloon. That building in the front at right was for floral displays.

The Prattsville Cornet Band at the Fairgrounds. Photograph circa 1904.

Left to right: (front row) Harley Parker, Joe Enderlin, Seymore Miller, Claude White; (back row) Sheridan Tompkins, Lyman Alberti, Benny Merwin, James Brennen, Dave Brandow, Stewart Tuttle, Charles Becker, Austin Hammel, John Becker, James McWilliams.

Schoharie Valley. Postcard circa 1902. Here we are looking east over the fertile valley of the Schoharie Kill at the turn of the century. As in other panoramas of the mountaintop at this time, most of the trees are gone and the valley has become a prosperous farming and dairying community. What seem to be lines crisscrossing the landscape are stone walls dividing neighbors' pasturelands.

The farmhouse in the lower left corner is that of P.K. Salpsbury, a lawyer and insurance agent in Prattsville in the late 1860s. In the center of the photograph (not visible), running left to right is the Batavia Kill, which joins the Schoharie Kill in the vicinity of the Big Rock.

This photograph was taken by Harvey Peckham from Pratt's Rock, where Zadock Pratt had his accomplishments immortalized in stone. Over the last thirty years of his life, Pratt hired stone carvers to begin depicting his businesses, his family and his favorite animals in raised relief and painted white for all to see and remember him by.

And today there is indeed a lot of remembering to do in Prattsville.

Photograph circa 1910. As we enter the village of Prattsville, we first come upon this buggy and fine pair of horses driven by Vernon Chatfield. Out for a ride, Vernon is passing the Prattsville Methodist Church. The church was built in 1834 on land donated by Zadock Pratt.

At one time Vernon ran heavy equipment for the State Highway Department. In later years Vernon and his wife opened the Pratt Rock Tea Room across from the barrier dam.

Postcard circa 1907. Nearly across from the Methodist Church, we find the Pleasant Home Cottage. Judging by the number of guests in front, this must have been a very inviting Main Street boardinghouse. It was owned and operated by Mr. and Mrs. Andrew Carmen for a long time. Andrew was in the trucking business many years and, by 1920, he bought out the trucking business of W.C and C.V. White and continued that business with three trucks.

Photograph circa 1910. Dairy farming was still very prosperous around 1920. Here we find Willie Simon of Prattsville, who has just delivered a wagonload of milk to the Prattsville Creamery. He is now returning the empty cans to their respective owners. Traveling east along Main Street, Willie is passing the house that was the home of B. Griffin in 1867.

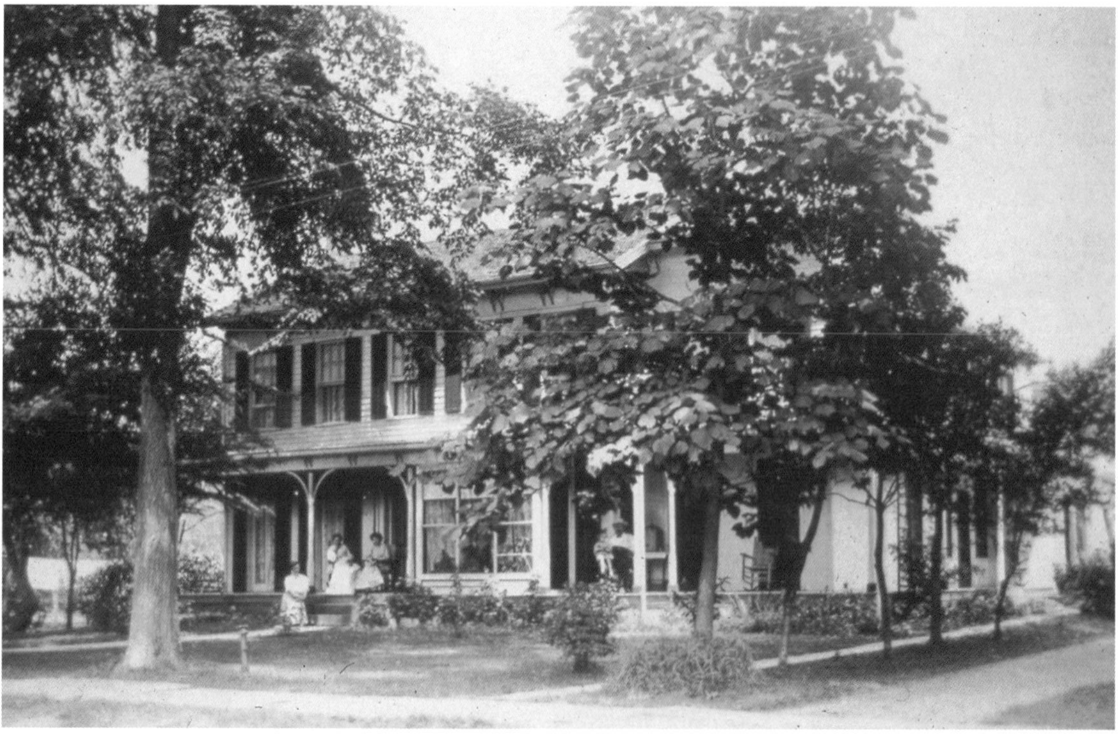

Photograph circa 1910. This lovely large building, today completely restored, was the former Presiding Elders Home for retired Methodist ministers. The Windham and Prattsville circuit was organized in 1834 with Reverend Thomas S. Barrett as the first minister of the Prattsville Methodist Church. The residence is located three houses west of the church.

JUNE 1879.

It is surprising what a crowd of people are called out on Saturday evenings, at Prattsville, to hear the band play. Generally two or three fights and occasional arrest adds spice to the amusement.

Grace Episcopal Church. Photograph circa 1895. Before 1843 Prattsville residents attended services in either the Windham or Ashland Episcopal churches. As the congregation grew, there was a need for having their own church in Prattsville. Zadock Pratt donated the land, and $2,000 was raised to construct this impressive Gothic church. It was built using wood from the hemlock trees cut down for their bark, which was used in the tanning process.

The church flourished for about forty years before closing and eventually being taken down. It was located on the site of the present Prattsville Diner.

Brookside Cottage. Postcard circa 1915. Across from Grace Episcopal Church stood the D.M. Frayer house in 1867. In later years Zack Carmen purchased the property and enlarged the house into a boardinghouse called Brookside Cottage. Carmen ran a trapping and sporting goods store in the mid-1920s while his wife ran the boardinghouse.

Photograph circa 1948. Many years after the Grace Episcopal Church was taken down, Orlan Howard built this gas station around 1935 on the church site. Donald Morse also ran the station at one time. By the mid-1960s, Christopher Hellmer came to town and built the present-day diner and bakery.

Elm Tree Inn. Photograph circa 1915. This large house was erected circa 1830 and was the home of A.J. Churchill in 1867. The house was originally closer to the turnpike, but was moved back to create a large front lawn for the new boardinghouse it was to become. By the 1940s it became a bar and rooming house run by Claude Ferris. Joel Perry ran a bar here in the 1950s. Later the building was leased out as a pizza parlor, laundromat and liquor store. It was located on the site of the Great American supermarket parking lot.

Lutz Villa. Postcard circa 1910. This home, built for the first minister of Grace Episcopal Church in 1845, might be one of the earliest houses built on the mountaintop to be used as a manse. It is a fine example of the gingerbread Gothic style and is built in the shape of a cross. Some time after the Episcopal Church closed, the manse became the private home of Edward Lutz and his son Sayer. Today it is once again a manse, but for the Dutch Reformed Church.

Prattsville Village Academy, District 2. Photograph circa 1916. Built in 1842 by the community, with substantial help from Zadock Pratt, this is a very formal-looking two-story brick building with a wooden veranda all around the second floor. Classes were taught through the eighth grade. In 1849 tuition for an eleven-week term was \$3–\$5. If room and board was necessary, it cost \$1.50 per week. Sometime around the 1920s a fire destroyed the entire upper level of the school and it became a one-story building. Even after centralization of the district in the 1930s, this school continued to be used, on and off, until 1951. The school was then closed and the building remained vacant until the mid-1980s, when it was used as a courthouse. The Town of Prattsville took over the building in 1989 for use as the Town Hall and town offices.

Zadock Pratt Homestead. Photograph circa 1914. By age thirty-four, Zadock Pratt, already a very successful businessman, came to Schohariekill to begin his new endeavor in the tanning industry. In 1828 he began construction on this stately house in the center of town. With many additions over the years, the house became a grand home. The addition on the left was the Prattsville Bank, but was added on to the house in 1843. The bank had been located where the present post office stands today.

The house stayed in the family for many years. Subsequent owners began to separate the house into several apartments in the mid-1900s. The building began to deteriorate, and concerned citizens took notice. To begin to preserve the house, Brayton Tompkins and Hilda Mosemen, along with the support of the Prattsville Chamber of Commerce, saved the deteriorating house and began the Zadock Pratt Museum. Much of the history of the Pratt family, as well as the history of the town, has been displayed here for many years. In 1975–76 the house was completely restored to its mid-nineteenth-century glory and is a lasting asset to the Town of Prattsville.

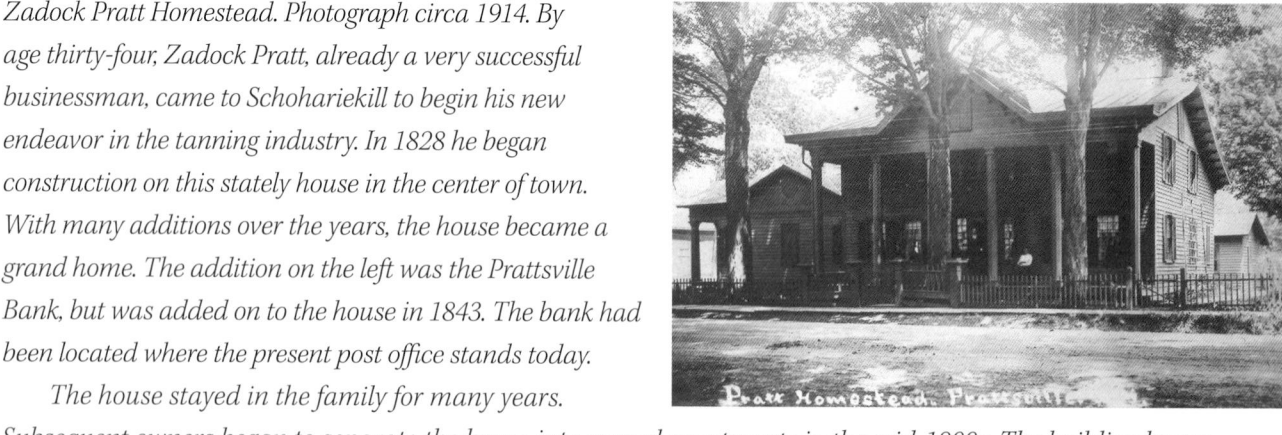

Photograph circa 1905. The beauty of Prattsville is readily apparent when looking at this wonderful Main Street photograph from the early twentieth century. The wide roadway, the bluestone sidewalks, the beautiful maple trees lining the sidewalks, and the stepped carriage block speak to the love and care and pride the residents of Prattsville took in their community in maintaining what had been bestowed upon them by their illustrious benefactor Zadock Pratt.

We are looking east along the turnpike. This family is standing across the road from Pratt's house. You can see Elm Tree Inn and the Grace Episcopal Church on the left.

JULY 1865.

The population of the town of Prattsville according to the late census, is 1,530. Of the Village of Red Falls, 180, and of the Village of Prattsville, 675. The town has furnished 100 men for the army, of whom four have been killed in battle, three starved by the Rebels, ten died of sickness contracted in the service, and eight have deserted. The oldest inhabitant in town is William Shoemaker, age 90 years.

Prattsville Band. Photograph circa 1910. As in almost every hamlet and town on the mountaintop, music was a big part of children's education and upbringing. It was a welcome form of entertainment and a break from the long days of school, work, and raising a family. After several attempts, a formal band was established in Prattsville around 1883. Smart-looking uniforms, a drum major and shiny brass instruments were a welcome sight parading down Main Street on the 4th of July or at family picnics or reunions. These gentlemen are standing in front of what was the Prattsville bank.

The bank was established in 1843. This was another profitable endeavor for Zadock Pratt and the citizenry as the town continued to grow and prosper. Over its nine-year existence, the bank doubled Pratt's investment. Pratt even printed money with his own likeness on it.

Left to right: (front row) Sanford Tompkins, Harley Parker, Orville Hummel, Sherwood Tompkins, Claude White, Jim Stickles and John Becker; (second row) Dey Brandow, James McWilliams, Lloyd Sutton, George Heming, Benny Merwin, Jim Brenan, Austin Hummel, Joe Enderlin and Charles Snyder.

Malden G. Marsh House. Photograph circa 1910. Prosperity is evident in the construction of this fine house by Zadock Pratt circa 1840. One of the early residents was Mr. T. Montgomery. By 1873 the Malden Marsh family lived here.

Several newspapers had their beginnings over a twenty-year period in the mid-1880s. One of the earliest was the Baptist Library, *a periodical paper started by Levi L. and R.H. Hill in 1843. In 1845 the paper moved down the road to Lexington. Levi L. Hill, besides being a printer, was a preacher and a photographer from Little Westkill. Levi was a pioneer in the development of color photography; samples of his color photographs are in the National Archives.*

Another early paper was the Prattsville Advocate, *started in 1846 by John Hackstaff. This paper operated for twelve years. As the* Advocate *closed doors, the* Prattsville News *was started by J.G. Gregory. Malden purchased the paper in 1864. Malden also purchased the old tailor shop just west of his house and began publishing his newspaper there, and continued to do so for about sixty years. Earlier, circa 1856, that building housed a shop called The Boston Cash Store.*

Photograph circa 1908. Here is another view of the beautiful maple tree-lined Main Street, looking west from in front of Pratt's house. Creamery Lane is to the immediate left, and Washington Street to the right. In the mid-1800s residents took pride in their own establishments and the appearance of Main Street in general. The building on the left is Montgomery & Sage's dry goods store. On the extreme right is Joseph Platner's Drug Store, located on the northwest corner of Washington Street.

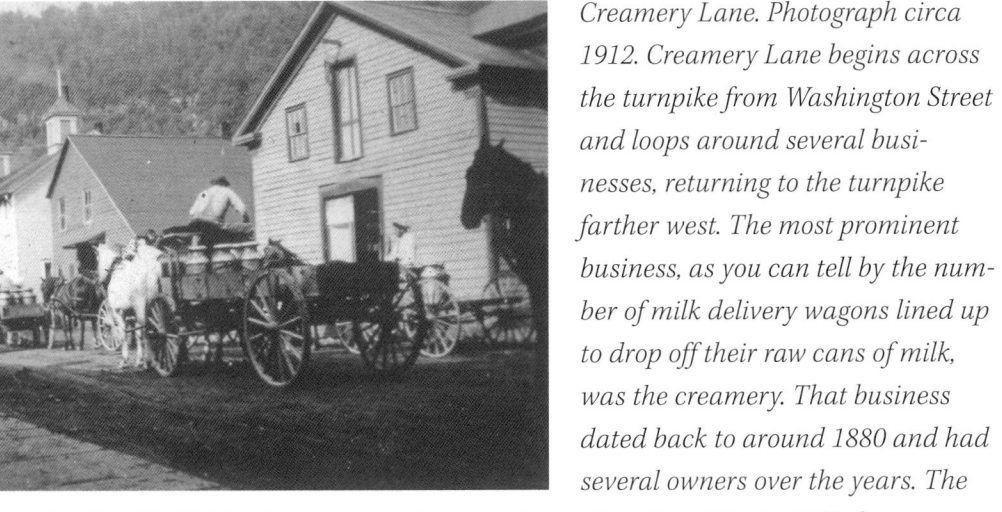

Creamery Lane. Photograph circa 1912. Creamery Lane begins across the turnpike from Washington Street and loops around several businesses, returning to the turnpike farther west. The most prominent business, as you can tell by the number of milk delivery wagons lined up to drop off their raw cans of milk, was the creamery. That business dated back to around 1880 and had several owners over the years. The early creamery was once owned by Mr. Sheffield, who ran several creameries in New York City. In 1911 the creamery incorporated with Elmer Krieger as president of the new company. The local citizens had purchased back what they renamed The Prattsville Co-Operative Creamery Company. Also purchased from Mr. Sheffield were icehouses and several acres of land, totaling $12,000. The creamery began receiving 10,000 pounds of milk a day. Much of the cream was shipped to New York City.

Other businesses on this road were Ed Lutz's Feed Store, Pat Jordan's Blacksmith Shop, Fred Jordan's Bottling and Ice Cream Works, and Mr. Arnold's Feed Store.

Photograph circa 1916. Here we are looking into one of the last blacksmith shops on the mountaintop. In 1916 there were still many farmers working the land with horses and plows and wagons, requiring shoes for the horses and hardware and rims for the wagon wheels. Patrick Jordan was still shoeing horses well into the 1930s. Jordan's shop and house were located near the far end of Creamery Lane close to Young's Agway store of the present day.

May 1870.

While in Prattsville one day, we called on the venerable Colonel Zadock Pratt. We found the Colonel ensconced in his favorite arm chair, apparently enjoying himself. The Colonel's housekeepers were busily engaged in cleaning house, and things were scattered promiscuously about. This did not prevent us from having a social chat with this veteran philanthropist and recipient of many merited honors. The Colonel has a nice residence and is surrounded by all the comforts, calculated to make his last hours pleasant and comfortable. In the course of his eventful life he has given to public and private charities about $1,000,000. We caught a glimpse of the fifth Mrs. Pratt, who was attired in a plain suit, and was evidently intently engaged in assisting in, and superintending the cleaning operations. The Colonel will be 80 years old on October 30. Still he appears to hold his own.

Photograph circa 1900. This view looks east along Main Street from just west of the present firehouse to Creamery Lane. In 1867 the larger building, center right, was D.R. Ferris's market/grocery store. The building with porch columns in left center was built by Erskine Laraway in 1863. It was then sold to Montgomery & Sage as a dry goods store. The building next to the west of Laraway's is another mercantile store. The prosperity of Prattsville is evident from the number, size and variety of businesses along Main Street. All of the buildings pictured are gone. The Fireman's Hall and Firehouse now occupy the site of the three middle buildings.

N. & L. E. ERKSON,

GENERAL MERCHANDISE

Staple and Fancy Dry Goods a Specialty.

Also Dealers in

FLOUR, FEED, GRAIN.

Store and Warerooms, Main St., (opp. Prattsville House), PRATTSVILLE, N. Y.

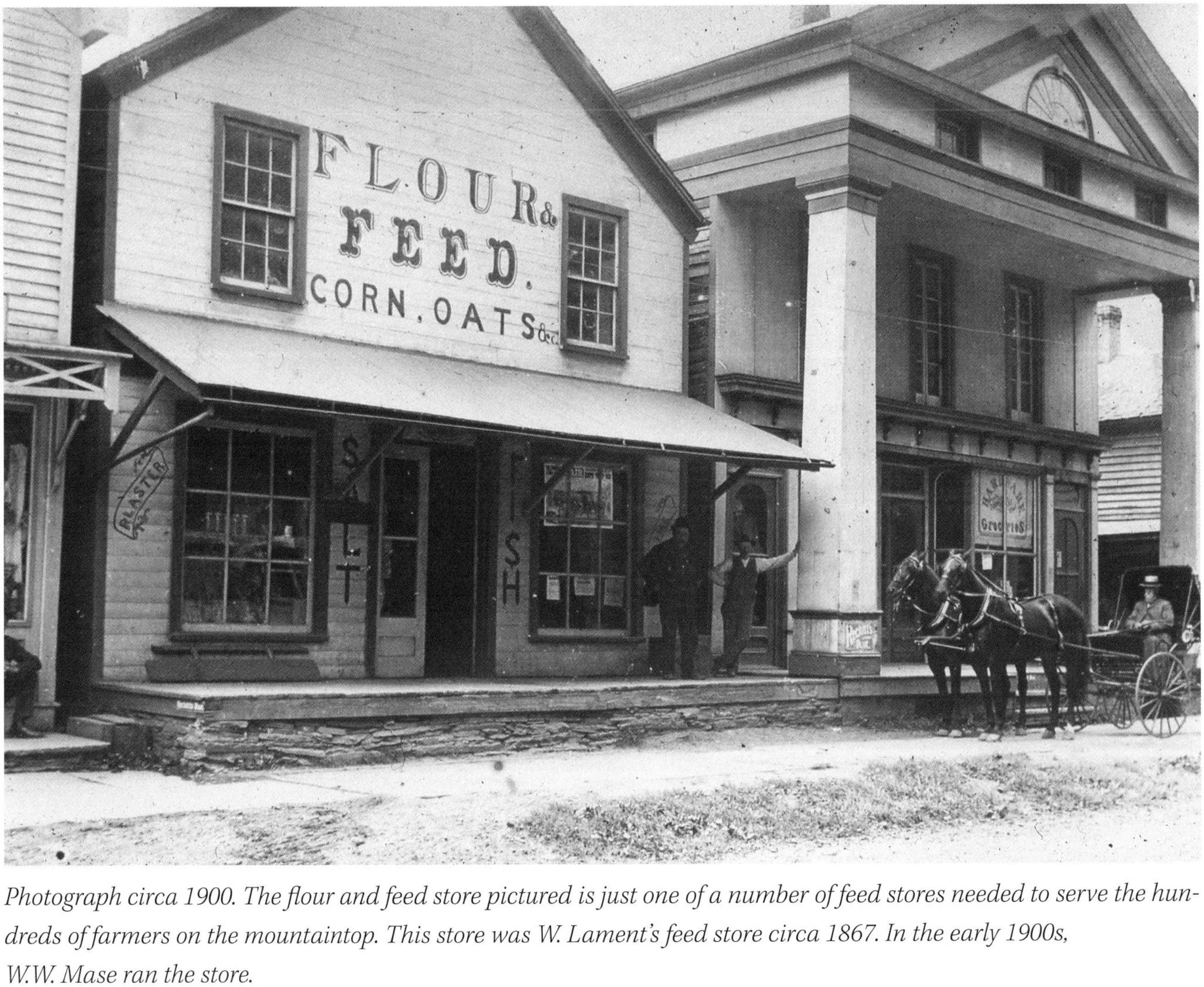

Photograph circa 1900. The flour and feed store pictured is just one of a number of feed stores needed to serve the hundreds of farmers on the mountaintop. This store was W. Lament's feed store circa 1867. In the early 1900s, W.W. Mase ran the store.

The large building to the right has always been a commercial enterprise. It is commonly referred to as the Opera House because silent movies were shown here in the very early 1900s. There was most likely also a stage on the second floor for small productions. This is probably the building that prominent businessman John Erkson purchased in 1876 and completely remodeled for his mercantile trade. At various times there was a barber shop, grocery store, hardware store, butcher shop, ice cream shop, pool hall and a hotel run by Mr. Star Mase on the premises. In 1938 the building was taken down and moved to Roxbury.

Layman's Bar and Restaurant. Photograph circa 1949. After many years as a dry goods store, in the mid-1940s Frank Layman purchased this building and converted it into a popular bar and restaurant. In 1953 the building burned beyond repair, and the lot remained empty for many years. In 1972 Claude Lutz bought the lot and put up a new building for his insurance business. That building served the community until 2011 when it was swept away by Tropical Storm Irene. The building on the extreme right, after being a dry goods store for many years, became the Prattsville Masonic Hall. In the mid-1950s a brick-front structure replaced the old wooden Masonic Hall. Sometime in the mid-1940s Chet Jordan, son of Pat Jordan the town blacksmith, built the small structure between Layman's and the Masonic Hall. It became an ice cream parlor and pool hall. Behind these buildings on Creamery Lane was Fred Jordan's Bottling and Ice Cream Works.

Photograph circa 1907. Cars had been on the road for a few years now, but in 1907 the mountaintop was still in the horse-and-buggy era. This large touring car with its several well-dressed passengers is parked near the Prattsville House, where it drew a large crowd of men and boys to come out to inspect this fine vehicle. The condition of the roads is evident on the fenders and tires of the car.

FEBRUARY 1870.

A young lady was frozen to death, while out sleigh riding with a young man. A man who can't keep a woman from freezing should be punished to the full extent of the law.

Photograph circa 1896. De Lisser, Picturesque Catskills. *One of the most prominent buildings on Main Street was the Prattsville House in the center of town. Built circa 1830 by Zadock Pratt, the hotel had numerous owners over the years—J. DeNoyelles in 1857, J.T. Huggins in 1859, Dinegar and Smith in 1860, George Martin in 1867 and Dwight Miller in 1901. The hotel still operates today. Two other Prattsville hotels operating in the mid-1800s, but rarely mentioned, were the Central Hotel, owned by Henry Jordon, and the Cyrus Smith Esq. Hotel.*

Dry Goods Store. Photograph circa 1915. This was built by Zadock Pratt as a store for his workers circa 1835. In early days this was the Tyler Millinery Store. The attic was used for a dance hall, and the unique fanlight attic window was designed to call attention to the dance hall. In this picture we see Etta Curtis Smith standing outside her dry goods store on Main Street. By the mid-1940s Pete Layman lived here.

Gray Gables Cottage. Photograph circa 1910. What seems apparent is that this house was once two smaller houses that were joined together. These were just two of the over one hundred houses that Zadock Pratt built for his many hundreds of employees that were running the tannery and other mills in Prattsville in 1835. After the houses were joined together, Will Rudolph opened the Gray Gables boardinghouse. In later years it was the home of Frank and Mary Dresser.

Mail Coach. Photograph circa 1906. Here we find Willis Lutz with his fine-looking rig ready to deliver mail in the Prattsville area. Lutz was a hard-working, industrious young man. At one time he worked for his brother Ed at his feed store on Creamery Lane. Then, in 1911, Willis and Claude C. White bought the corner store (at the corner of Washington Street and Route 23) from druggist Joe Platner for $2,500. They called their dry goods store the Store of Quality, and it was run by Willis while White continued his insurance business.

Reformed Dutch Church. Photograph circa 1906. Organized in 1802 by Rey Lopaugh, the first church was constructed in 1804. A fire in 1835 destroyed the church, and a new building was erected with the aid of Zadock Pratt. This beautiful church still has its original windows and box pews. In 1972 the church was completely restored. It served faithfully for 178 years until August 2011, when Tropical Storm Irene devastated the lower part of the church and the fellowship hall. Restoration efforts continue today.

Platner's Feed Store. Photograph circa 1910. This large building almost directly across from the Dutch Reformed Church was erected on the site of Pratt's Grist Mill, which later became a hat mill. The mill was carried away by a freshet in 1869. The new building was constructed by Mr. Rudolph, who continued his hat business until 1880. Later the building was used for carding rolls and making cider. By 1894 there was a feed store here with a good bakery in the basement. Chester Platner took over the feed store and ran it for many years until he died in 1932. Shortly after, the building was taken down. In the late 1940s Harold Powell operated a gas station here. Many years later an antique store was on this site.

Elm Tree Filling Station. Photograph circa 1930. This was built in 1925 by Thomas O'Hara, the first O'Hara to come to Prattsville. This was the site of the old livery stables used by the inn across the road. It was next to the old blacksmith shop by the bridge. At one time this gas station was one of four operating on Main Street. It was the last gas station in Prattsville to close, but it continued on as a garage, as it still does today. Along the right side of the station, you would have seen "New York State's Largest Elm Tree." By 1950 this 300-year-old tree measured 20 feet 3 inches in circumference and had a shade span of 150 by 130 feet. It was cut down in August 1955 because of the spread of Dutch elm disease.

Photograph circa 1896. De Lisser, Picturesque Greene County. *We have now reached the site of a very early covered bridge, built circa 1830. When the covered bridge washed away, residents for a time had to ford the Schoharie Kill on foot. A temporary bridge was constructed in 1862 that served until the iron bridge pictured was built in 1870. The building in the picture is the old blacksmith shop, built circa 1862.*

Fowler House. Photograph circa 1890. One of the most magnificent and historical homes in Prattsville is the Charles Fowler House, located nearly opposite the bridge on West Main Street. It was originally the John and Martins Laraway Inn, built circa 1785. John operated one of the earliest gristmills in the area. The inn served the traveling public for about 130 years until Tom O'Hara came to Prattsville in 1919, built his first garage across the road in 1925, and purchased the inn as a residence. The O'Hara family still resides there today.

The inn changed hands several times over the many years it operated. It was C. Smith's Hotel in 1856, C.E. Richtmyre's Hotel in 1867 and the Charles Fowler House circa 1896.

September 1870.

Work in clearing out the bed of the Huntersfield stream is being pushed rapidly forward, the ladies of the Sewing Society having donated $40. "Long live the Ladies." Prattsville.

Photograph circa 1906. This beautiful lady is Edith Peckham. Edith was the sister of Harvey Peckham, a local photographer who took many of the iconic old photographs that one sees of early Prattsville circa 1910. Edith was married to Warren Becker, a foreman on the State Highway Department. They lived in an old house just east of the Reformed Dutch Church Manse and took in boarders for many years.

Postcard circa 1905. Nearly opposite the bridge and two doors down from the Fowler House, we come to the Wayside Cottage. This very comfortable-looking boardinghouse must have been a good place to eat, as three of the signs out front speak of the food served inside. There are also tables and chairs on the porch. This was Mrs. Jordan's house circa 1867.

Devasego Falls. Photograph circa 1900. The popularity of Devasego Falls is very evident in this picture. The falls were spectacular, 50 feet high and 125 feet wide, and were considered a miniature Niagara Falls. They were located just over the town line on the road to Gilboa. Tourists came from miles around to view these magnificent falls. They were originally known as the Owlfleck, named after an Indian living in the area. There is a substantial inn across the Gilboa road that is associated with the falls, called Devasego Inn. Notice the wooden stairs on the left provided by the inn's owner for easier access to the bottom of the falls.

In 1926 the Schoharie Creek was dammed farther down the creek to create a reservoir for New York City water. The waterfalls and the old town of Gilboa are now under this reservoir.

Photograph circa 1914. Ten years ago I placed this photograph in the Windham Journal *asking if anyone could identify these girls—a real longshot. Two weeks later a letter came to me from Saint Petersburg, Florida. The lady who responded, Dr. Frances Persons Huntley, said that she was the little girl on right, at age one and a half. The girl on the left is Lillian Deyo of Lexington. The photographs were taken by Elroy Hand, one of the first people in Lexington to have a camera.*

Frances was ninety years old when she wrote back to me. I quote the last sentence of her letter: "To think I was considering canceling my subscription to the Journal!! *Not Yet!!"*

Photograph circa 1908. Just over the line in West Prattsville, you enter the small farming community of Johnson Hollow, where the days were long and farming the rocky soil was very arduous. One of the families that lived here was the Ives. Here we see Parker Ives and his family behind their house, cutting and splitting firewood for the long hard winter to come. With the help of his sons and neighbors, Parker ran a sawmill operation on his numerous acres of farmlands and woods.

JULY 1882.

Prattsville complains of a nuisance the likes of which Windham has long endured—too many neat cattle on the sidewalks. The cattle may be neat enough but the walks are not. If those who have occasion to drive animals through the village would there by contribute much to decency and the comfort of pedestrians; nor would they exceed the demands of duty. We have fine walks but their usefulness is often much impaired by their barnyard characteristics.

Huntersfield School District #7, "The Weed District." Glass negative, circa 1905. This handsome one-room schoolhouse is located in the most northerly section of Prattsville Township, in Huntersfield, known as the "Weed District" because of the large number of families with large numbers of children living in this district.

Left to right: (children in front row) Lyle Conine, Cyrus Tompkins, Jay Conine, Essie Cammer, Mildred Cammer, Ruth Cammer, Reverend Phillip's daughter.

Note the separate entrances for girls and boys, which was typical in the nineteenth century.

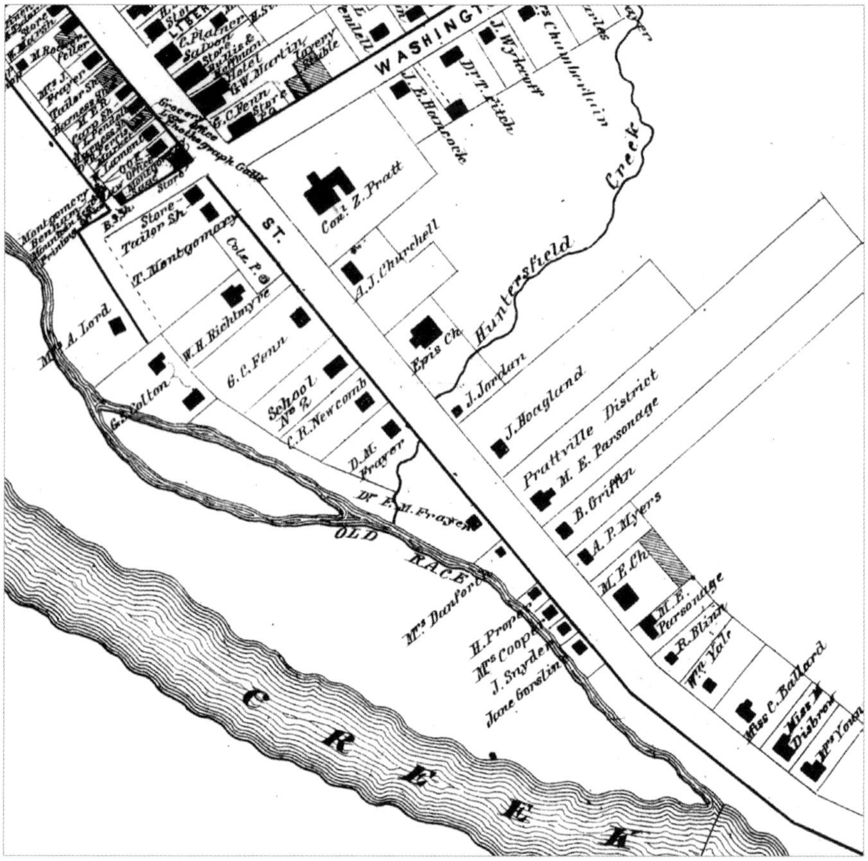

Left: East end of Main Street, Prattsville; below: West end of Main Street, Prattsville, 1867.

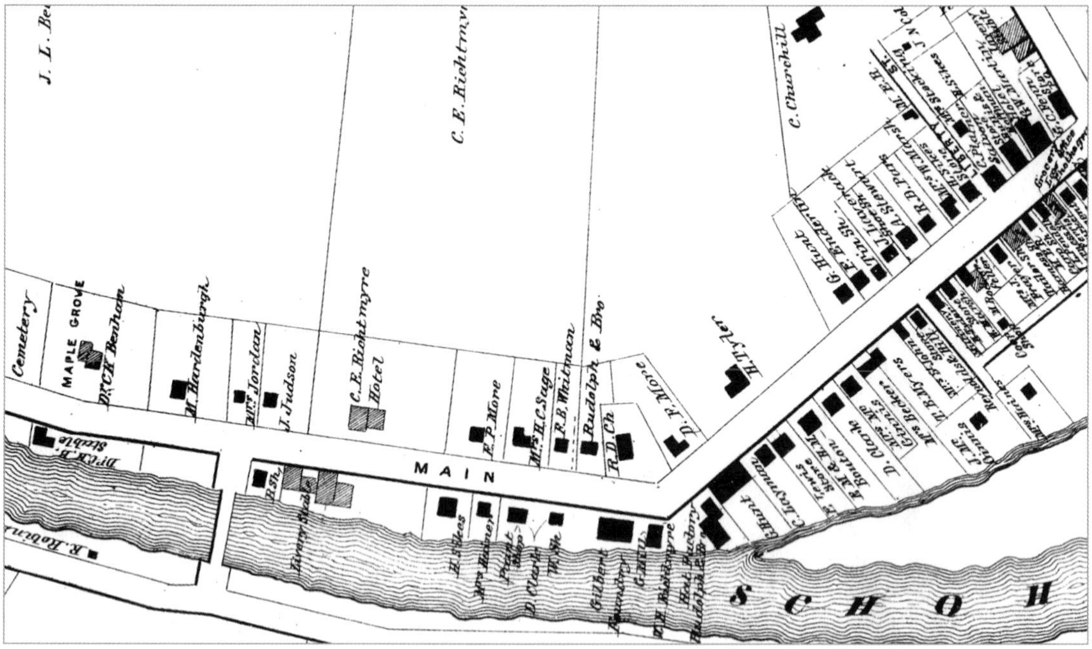

The Gem of the Catskills

Windham Village in the 1930s and 1940s

It is now 1935, and this Mohican chief is still promoting the virtues of his native land. While the many industries of the past are now gone, tourism is still thriving. Thousands of people are flocking to the dozens of fine boardinghouses in Windham and surrounding towns to partake of the beauty of the mountains. For four months of the year, the streets are bustling with visitors, with local merchants striving to meet their every need. The other eight months of the year, Windham is a sleepy little village, like most others in the Catskills. During the war years, local merchants still provided most of life's necessities. There was Morse's and Jacob's grocery stores, Miller Brothers department store, the Brockett and Strong hardware store, Don Crandell's gas station and garage, a lumber yard and two doctors, along with other merchants and professionals.

Pamphlet, circa 1935. The horse-and-buggy days are gone. The horseless carriages are now invading this Mohican chief's hunting grounds of old.

In the 1950s and 1960s, Windham was still the place to be in the summer. Upon leaving town to return to the city, no one, especially children, left without a souvenir. Indian tom-toms, hatchets, bow and arrows, rifles and headdresses were the rage. Anything with an Indian or black bear on it was a delight for young and old. Today these kinds of souvenirs are hard to come by.

Many residents of Windham will look at the following photos and remember the people and businesses mentioned and the buildings that are no longer there. I am now of the age that finds reminiscing a fond pastime. I hope to continue collecting these old photos and then pass them on to future generations. There will never be a shortage of local tales, humorous anecdotes and family histories in the making to pass on to the future, for history begets more history and there is no end.

The Kopper Kettle. Photograph circa 1940. What was a small farmhouse in 1910 has been transformed into the Kopper Kettle Tea Room and Gift Shoppe by Mr. Thomas St. John, owner of the Silver Lake property in East Windham. In 1916 it was sold to George and Ida Chamberlain, who first opened it as a restaurant. Later they built The Lodge. Other owners over the years were Mr. and Mrs. William Lutz and Dr. and Mrs. Frank Haner.

By 1955 the tea room days were over, and Edward and Cynthia Holmok purchased the business from the Lutz family. They remodeled the building and opened the Kopper Kettle Bar and Grill and a motel. The bar became very popular, and Ed's son Kevin and his wife Claudia changed the name to The Brooklyn Bridge. This became a hot spot to frequent year-round. Kevin retired from the business in 2010, and the new owners are Don and Lisa Muccilli.

Kessel's The Shebang. Photograph circa 1940. This was a very popular watering hole in Windham. It was owned by Charlie Kessel and located at the foot of Old Road. I remember being allowed into The Shebang at a young age, but only as far as the pinball machine. My twin sister Carol and I could play there for hours. The Shebang was replaced by Thetford's Pleasant View Lounge in 1959. That restaurant was managed by Richard and Patricia Thetford Pelham and was a popular spot for many years. Owner Charlie Kessel stands on the left, and my father, Clarence E. Tompkins, on the right.

August 1941.

Dorville C. Gifford will open a radio shop in the Corner Grocery building on Main Street [Munson's] where he will repair radios and Allied electrical appliances.

Windham Diner. Negative, circa 1950. This diner was built by Thomas Constance in 1949 on a site near Creamery Pond on East Main Street. While popular for a while and offering great food, there were just not enough patrons to sustain it along with all the other popular eateries in town. The diner closed in 1952 and was moved to a new location off the mountain.

Saint Theresa's Roman Catholic Church. Negative, circa 1948. The church was built by C.D. Brockett, Seymour Cooke and J.H. Jordan, all of whom worked for the Govern Bros. contractors of Stamford. Father George Murray was the first priest. Before St. Theresa's was built, Catholic services were held at Olcliff in East Windham and the Osborn House in Brook Lynne. This beautiful church burned in 1962 and was replaced with a larger brick building and rectory.

Ruth Campbell, Age Seven. Photograph circa 1910. Born and raised in Oak Hill, Ruth married Milton Brandow and lived her adult life in Windham. Everyone remembers her daughter Rose Brandow Scattagood.

Brandow's Garage. Photograph circa 1945. Built circa 1933 by Ken Miner, this was just one of several garages on Main Street. It was sold to Milton Brandow in 1955, and then to Nelson Ohl in 1961, who continues to operate it today. Nelson changed the name to the Alpine Service Center, and it is the last remaining garage on Main Street.

The Windham Arms. Photograph circa 1945. This hotel was built on the site of the very early homestead of Colonel James Robertson, circa 1800. It was one of the finest farms in Windham. James's daughter Lydia married Abira Barney, and the farm was in the Barney family for many years. By 1880 Elbert Barney called his farm/guest house the Barney House. A succession of owners followed, including Watson Hall, Walter and Norma Soper in 1927, and Larry and Eleanor Lane in 1946. The Sopers named the house Windham Arms and operated it for nineteen years.

Then, for the next forty-eight years the Lanes ran the Windham Arms Hotel. It grew and flourished through their hard work and innovations. Many changes were made over the years to please their most finicky of guests. Along with their creative, hard-working, smiling and gracious daughter Claudia, they made the Windham Arms Hotel "The Aristocrat of Fine Hotels." Today the hotel is part of the Windham Mountain Resort, owned by Windham Mountain Partners.

Vining's Paint Store. Photograph circa 1936. Not long after Kissock & Coons moved their monument shop, William A. Conley opened a feed store here, one of many in town. In 1930 Conley leased part of the building to Walter Vining for a paint store, which Vining operated for many years. Conley added a gas pump, Socony Gas, in later years, and his was one of several places to get gas in town.

Main Street Windham in Front of Wallace Cammer & Lee Decker's Funeral Home. Negative, circa 1949. We find Wallace Cammer, on the left, and his assistant standing in front of the Cammer Decker Ambulance. Note the catchy logo, "Drive Safely / We Can Wait!" Behind them on the right is the large house of Maurice and Marie Sullivan. Maurice was a lawyer in town.

Photograph circa 1942. This beautiful little girl in her nurse's outfit has just arrived at her home after being out selling Girl Scout cookies. This is Stephanie Sullivan, daughter of Maurice Sullivan.

Avery's Drug Store. Photograph circa 1925. After thirty-six years in business, Anson R. Mott sold his drug store to Harry "Doc" Avery in 1917. Avery ran the drugstore in the same helpful and gracious manner as had Mott, providing the finest drugs and medicines available. "Doc" retired in 1955 and sold the store to Lewis and Gwen Wakefield. They ran the drugstore for another thirty years, along with their son John and his wife Micky, in the same fine tradition. Bill and Mark Quackenbush purchased the store in November 1985.

Photograph circa 1948. Harry Avery inside his always well-stocked drugstore, ready to serve his loyal customers.

C. C. CAMMER

TONSORIAL PARLOR AND POOL ROOM

Confectionery, Tobacco & Cigars

Main Street WINDHAM, N. Y.

Photograph circa 1948. This snowy scene finds Donald and Raymond Thompson removing the snow from in front of their plumbing and heating business on the corner of Mill Street and Main Street. Welcome Moore's feed and grain business was in the rear of this building.

The Blue Moon Luncheonette. Negative, circa 1948. Sometime around 1925, after the Patterson Bros. and Mr. Steadman retired from business, changes were made to their building. Steadman's Harness Shop was extended to match Patterson's store and became the town post office. Alvah Munson and Dennis Ferris opened their own grocery store, Munson's Corner Store, around 1925 in the right side of the building. They were still two separate buildings at this point.

In 1925 Clyde and Frances Adams bought the post office building and operated the very popular Blue Moon. After the corner store closed, the Blue Moon expanded into that part of the building. In later years the Blue Moon was run by Glen and Clara Jump, then Tom and Sue Stead, 1962–1970, and lastly, Karl and Joan Anis until February 1975, when it was completely destroyed by fire. The Blue Moon was a favorite early meeting and gathering spot for a 15¢ cup of coffee and the latest news of happenings around town. It was a tragic loss.

Today this is the site of Todaro's Salumeria.

Daytime Activity at the Corner of Mill Street and Main Street. Negative, circa 1940s. Munson's Corner Store is at center, and the Blue Moon is to the left.

Sokoll's Garage. Negative, circa 1948. From 1915 to 1938, Harold B. Moore ran the Windham Garage; he then sold the business to Mike and Lyle Sokoll. Their garage and Ford agency served the community for over fifty years. John La Vecchia took over the business and was the last auto dealer on Main Street before the building was transformed into a diner. The present owner is Nick Malegiannakis.

September 1943.

"Take it back!"—that milk bottle of course—to the corner grocery store or to the dairy that supplies your milk. Too many folks seem to forget and as a result the supply of milk bottles is low. Bottle manufacturers say they cannot turn out new ones fast enough to replace those not being returned. Nor can enough paper cartons be made to use in place of glass containers. It all boils down to this: If you want your milk, do your part and turn in the empty bottles.

Negative, circa 1949. This building, the former George Davis Central Hotel circa 1910, has now become the Village Inn, owned by John Matsos. Sometime in the mid-1950s Lyle and Peggy Sokoll purchased the building and continued the restaurant, calling it The Old Coach Inn. After about eight years in the restaurant business, Lyle decided that more parking for his busy garage and auto sales business was necessary, and The Old Coach Inn was torn down.

First TV's for Sale. Negative, circa 1948. It's ten PM on a warm summer night on Main Street, and we are outside Miller Bros. department store. Over one hundred citizens are gathered in front of the windows of Harold "Red" Bailey's Electronics Store to watch the first TV for sale in Windham.

Photograph circa 1948. Back in the 1950s one could find a barber shop in almost every town. Today, most men's haircuts are given at a local beauty salon. The old barber shop was a local gathering place to play checkers, watch TV, talk sports and, maybe, get a haircut. Here we find the locals watching a TV at Doug Goff's shop waiting for their 35¢ haircut. Goff was one of the most congenial gentlemen in Windham. The barber shop was located in the east end of Harry Brockett's store. The gentleman in the center, to the left of the register, is Harry Brockett.

Photograph circa 1955. This historic building, the early Masonic Hall, continues on with its many different enterprises. In 1954 Thomas Murtha purchased the building from the Katherine Cole estate and opened the very popular Sugar Bowl Ice Cream Parlor and Restaurant. This was a must stop after enjoying a movie at the Windham Theater behind the restaurant. In 1966 Mr. and Mrs. Stanley Stevens opened the Country Kitchen restaurant here. Subsequent owners were the Boylhart family. There was also a tack shop, owned by Russell Tompkins Jr., and later still, a flower shop. Today it is Coldwell Banker Reality.

Hotel Windham. Negative, circa 1950. In 1936 Frank Sarg, owner of the hotel, sold it to William Thetford, who changed the name to Hotel Windham. Under Thetford's capable management the Hotel Windham was considerably improved and modernized, with a modern cocktail lounge, a large dining room, and twenty-three rooms for guests. It was a big success for thirty-three years, then this historic building succumbed to fire on November 13, 1966. At the time of the fire, the owners were Frank and Margaret Burke. Today this is the site of Key Bank.

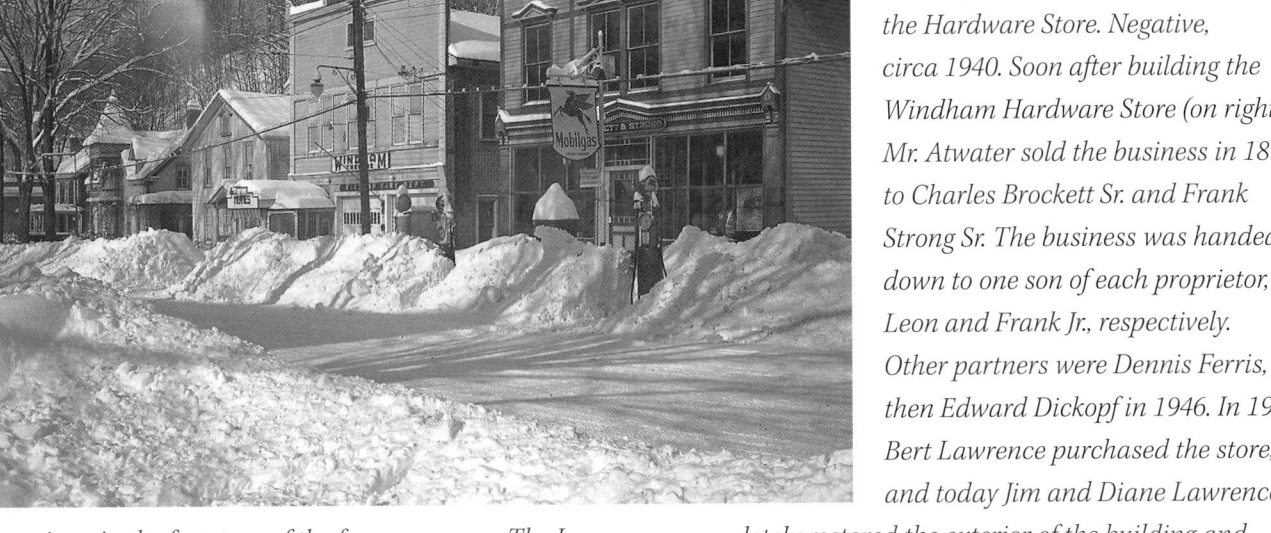

Looking West on Main Street near the Hardware Store. Negative, circa 1940. Soon after building the Windham Hardware Store (on right), Mr. Atwater sold the business in 1890 to Charles Brockett Sr. and Frank Strong Sr. The business was handed down to one son of each proprietor, Leon and Frank Jr., respectively. Other partners were Dennis Ferris, then Edward Dickopf in 1946. In 1968 Bert Lawrence purchased the store, and today Jim and Diane Lawrence continue in the footsteps of the former owners. The Lawrences completely restored the exterior of the building and carry an extensive line of hardware and household items.

In the center of this picture is the Fireman's Theatre, which began showing motion pictures circa 1914. The theater continued until 1949, when the Windham Theater opened across the road. The Windham Theater still operates today.

Greene County's Fireman's Convention Committee. Photograph circa 1935. This wonderful photograph is a Who's Who in Windham at that time, as firemen prepare for the 47th Annual Convention in Windham. Firemen from across the county got to trade stories and show off their oldest, finest and newest equipment.

Left to right: (standing) C.C. Cammer, D.A. Ferris, N.P. Willis, H.V. Newland, R.M. MacNaught, W.H. Moore, G.F. Morse, J.G. Mackey, and C.R. Tibbals; (seated) J.S. Patterson, A.C. Moore, M.J. Sullivan, R.G. Munson and G.W. Osborn Jr.

Morse's Fairlawn Grocery and Sam McCoubrey's Electronics Store. Photograph circa 1944. For fifty-three years the Morse family served the community in friendly fashion and was very popular with Windham-Ashland-Jewett students from the school across the road. McCoubrey sold electronic equipment and appliances for many years. The building was later used for the Friendly Red Door Loan Closet.

Inside McCoubrey's Electronics Store. Photograph circa 1944. McCoubrey, who was the local electrician, had this store for many years and sold radios, televisions and appliances. The building was just west of Windham National Bank.

Dick Quinn's Service Station. Photograph circa 1948. In earlier days this was Garraghan's Keystone Service Station, built originally by Austin R. Newcombe & Co. circa 1930. John Garraghan and Donald Crandell ran the service station. By 1936 Amos Post of Catskill purchased the station and leased it to Dick Quinn and later to his son Bill for many years. Dick built a newer house near Crandell's garage in 1949. Soon after, Amos Post built a new, modern service station between Dick's house and the old brick service station. That newer station later became a laundromat owned by Howard Thorp, and is today the Windham Liquor Store and Chinese Restaurant owned by Chuck and Lorraine McRoberts. The brick gas station is now Lorraine McRoberts's Garden of Stone Shop.

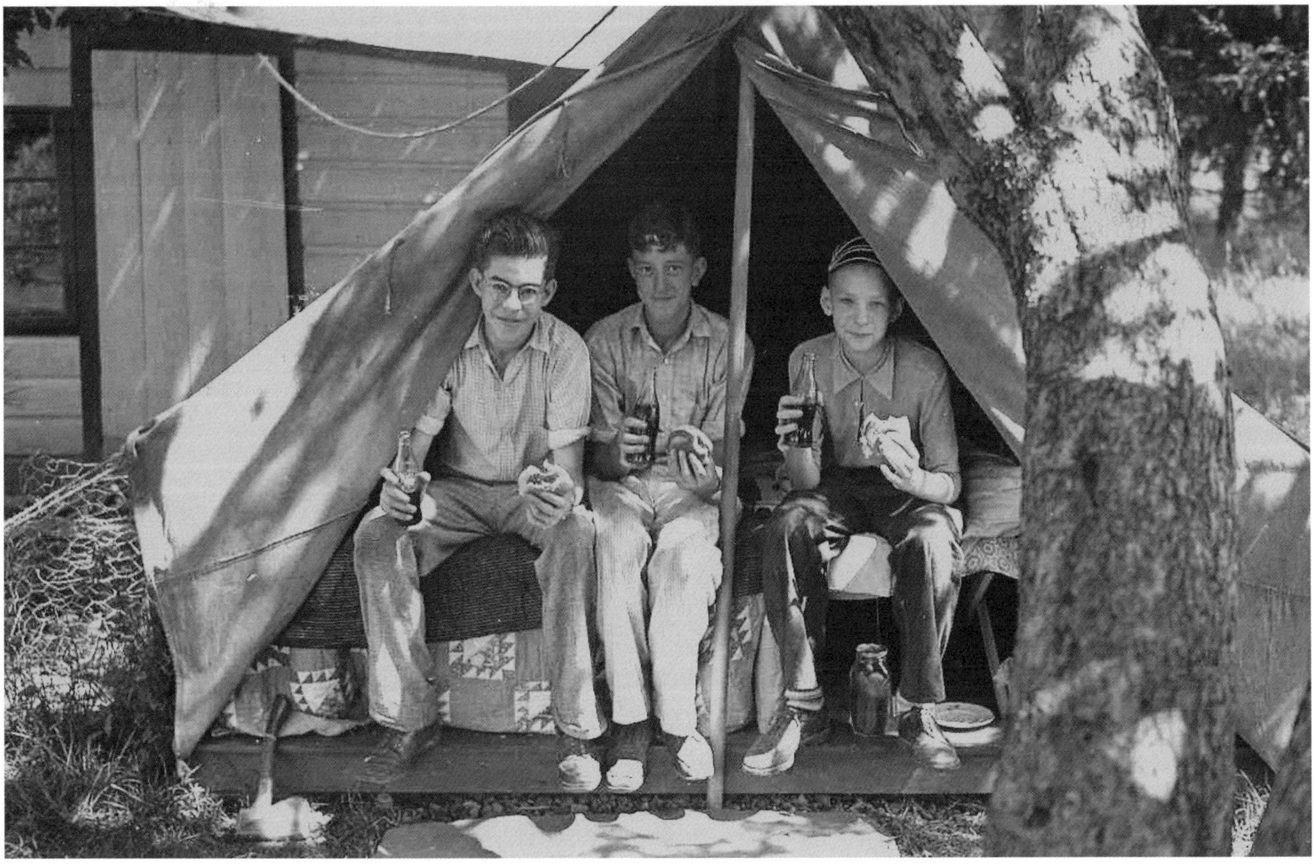

Photograph circa 1948. Here we find three Windham youths roughing it in the woods. Are those cots in the tent? Do they have hamburgers and cokes in their hands? I think they are in Wallace Cammer's backyard.

Left to right: Wallace Cammer, Robert Snyder, Richard Morse.

Crandell Bros. Garage. Negative, circa 1940s. On this site in the early 1840s was George Lamoreau's blacksmith and wheelwright shop. Sometime around 1851, Saint Paul's Chapel, a branch or mission of Trinity Church of Ashland, was built here. By 1871 it was a Free Methodist Church. The Shell oil tanks were part of the Catskill Mountain Petroleum Corp., started in 1928 by Audrey Moore. In later years his son-in-law Howard Thorp took over the business. Don Crandell ran the gas station for many years, followed by Greg Thorp from 1970–1984. When Howard Thorp retired, the property was turned over to the Windham Hose Company.

Cave Mountain Ski Resort. Photograph circa 1960. The first year of skiing in Windham was to usher in a transformation of the tourist industry in the northern Catskills. With the summer boardinghouse business in decline, it was hoped that skiing would be the driving engine of the tourist industry in the future.

Cave Mountain opened in the winter of 1960–61 with one tow rope run by a 1954 Buick motor and a Quonset hut for a base lodge. Town Supervisor C.D. Lane, Whit Mauzy and George Macomber were at the helm. Progress was slow, and after two seasons and with no money left, Walter Heffernan, a local lawyer, and Louis Wakefield, town pharmacist, leased the resort for the 1962–63 season, breathing new life into the ski area.

The Sheridan family took over in 1963 and, after a long stint as a private club, the ski area returned to the public sector in 1981 when purchased by Ski Round Top. Major improvements at the resort during the last thirty years have transformed Cave Mountain into the finest family oriented ski area in the Northeast. Presently the ski area is Windham Mountain Resort, owned by Windham Mountain Partners.

World War II Spotting Tower / Aircraft Warning Station. Negative, circa 1945. This was located on Indian Heights Road on the hill above the old bank building. Pictured are Sheridan Cammer and guests.

Windham Billboard. Photograph late 1940s. These welcome signs were erected in the late 1940s in Windham village and in Maplecrest. In very early written accounts, circa 1830, visitors referred to Old Windham as the "Gem of the Catskills." This aptly describes Windham today. Anson R. Mott chose to call his drugstore the Gem City Pharmacy to promote the virtues of Windham.

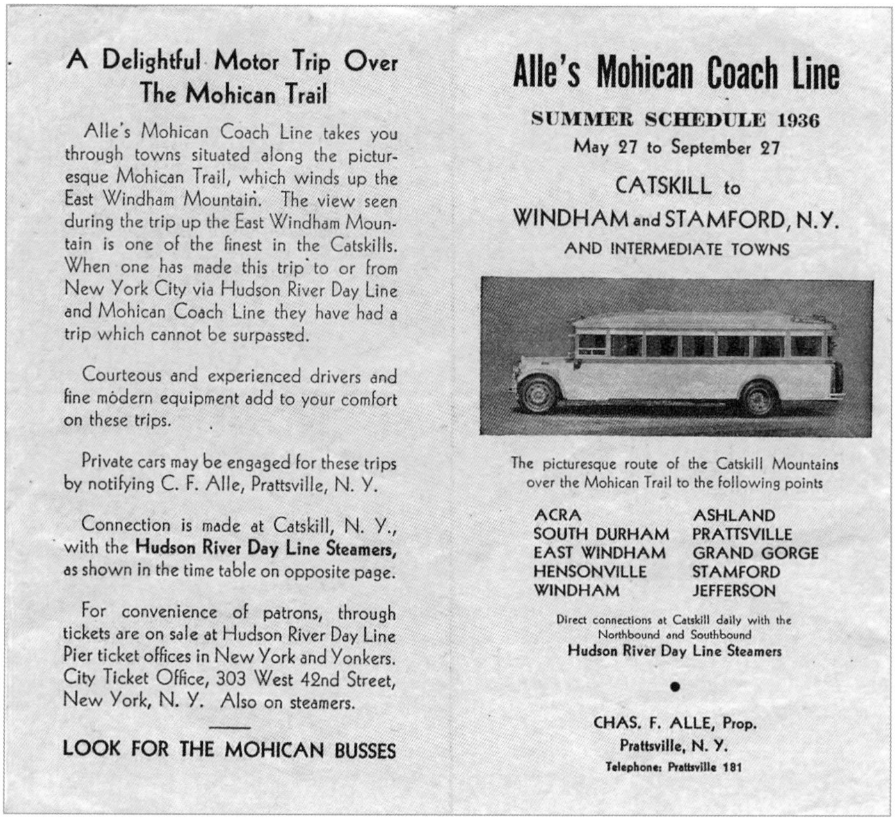

A Delightful Motor Trip Over The Mohican Trail

Alle's Mohican Coach Line takes you through towns situated along the picturesque Mohican Trail, which winds up the East Windham Mountain. The view seen during the trip up the East Windham Mountain is one of the finest in the Catskills. When one has made this trip to or from New York City via Hudson River Day Line and Mohican Coach Line they have had a trip which cannot be surpassed.

Courteous and experienced drivers and fine modern equipment add to your comfort on these trips.

Private cars may be engaged for these trips by notifying C. F. Alle, Prattsville, N. Y.

Connection is made at Catskill, N. Y., with the **Hudson River Day Line Steamers,** as shown in the time table on opposite page.

For convenience of patrons, through tickets are on sale at Hudson River Day Line Pier ticket offices in New York and Yonkers. City Ticket Office, 303 West 42nd Street, New York, N. Y. Also on steamers.

LOOK FOR THE MOHICAN BUSSES

Alle's Mohican Coach Line

SUMMER SCHEDULE 1936
May 27 to September 27

CATSKILL to
WINDHAM and STAMFORD, N.Y.
AND INTERMEDIATE TOWNS

The picturesque route of the Catskill Mountains over the Mohican Trail to the following points

ACRA — ASHLAND
SOUTH DURHAM — PRATTSVILLE
EAST WINDHAM — GRAND GORGE
HENSONVILLE — STAMFORD
WINDHAM — JEFFERSON

Direct connections at Catskill daily with the Northbound and Southbound
Hudson River Day Line Steamers

CHAS. F. ALLE, Prop.
Prattsville, N. Y.
Telephone: Prattsville 181

Alle's Mohican Coach Line. Pamphlet, circa 1936. It is 1936 and your Hudson River Day Line steamer has just arrived at Catskill Landing. There is no horse and carriage waiting to transport your party. That is fortunate, because although it may seem romantic to us today, it was hot, foul-smelling and dusty sitting behind four horses for a long carriage ride. Instead, Charles Alle is waiting for you in his new, comfortable, 24-passenger motor coach that will whisk you away to your mountain destination in a fraction of the time that it took in the horse-and-buggy days. Charles will stop at any one of the 100 hotels along the main road.

Visitors came here to relax and enjoy the amenities of their hotel, so they did not need their own car to get around. The hotels usually provided their own conveyances to transport their guests to surrounding tourist sites.

The Mohican Trail today still awaits your arrival with open arms, inviting you to embrace its staggering beauty, and the folks here are just as eager to welcome you in the same hospitable fashion as their forebears for generations past.

June 1867.

We presume we hazard nothing, when we venture the assertion that we have one of the most pleasant villages "in all the country round." Its location is romantic, its morals unexceptional and its people enterprising and intelligent. As a summer retreat from the busy turmoil of life, it cannot be excelled. The varying panorama of its mountain scenery furnishes a continued feast to the lover of beauty, which never pales upon the senses. If any discontented spirit is wandering to and fro, seeking for a terrestrial paradise, up on a small scale, let him come hither and we guarantee him entire satisfaction.

Sources Consulted

Beers, F.W. *Atlas of Greene County*. New York: F.W. Beers, A.D. Ellis & G.G. Soale, 1867.

Beers, J.B. *History of Greene County*. New York: J.B. Beers & Co., 1884.

Directory of the Ulster and Delaware Railroad. Newburgh, N.Y.: Thompson & Breed, 1890.

Gault. *Dear Old Greene County*. Catskill, N.Y.: Gault, 1915.

Greene County Historical Society. *Greene County Bicentennial Overview*. Hensonville, N.Y.: Black Dome Press, 2000.

Hitchcock, Elwood. *Big Hollow*. Hensonville, N.Y.: Black Dome Press, 1994.

Hitchcock, Elwood. *Hensonville*. Hensonville, N.Y. Black Dome Press, 1998.

Horne, Field. *The Greene County Catskills*. Hensonville, N.Y.: Black Dome Press, 1994.

Lorton, John. *Windham Articles in the Windham Journal*. 1886.

Millen, Patricia. *Bare Trees*. Hensonville, N.Y.: Black Dome Press, 1995.

Munson, Harold. *South Street Story*. Rochester, N.Y.: Mercury Productions, 2008.

Olsen, Margaret Radcliff. *East Windham*. East Windham, N.Y.: Marge Olsen, 1992.

Pons, Muriel. *Historic Prattsville, Pathways to the Past*. Prattsville Recreational Improvement Committee, 1995.

Prout, Rev. Henry Hedge. *Old Times in Windham*. Cornwallville, N.Y.: Hope Farm Press, 1970.

Thompson Family. *The Thompson House Pamphlet*. 1980.

Tompkins, Flora. *Ashland Academy*. Cornwallville, N.Y.: Hope Farm Press, 1979.

Wiles, Richard C. *Windham*. Cornwallville, N.Y.: Hope Farm Press, 1985.

Windham Journal. 1857–2013.

Index

A

B

N

O

P

R

S

T

U

V

W

Y